101 Creative Coconut Oil Uses

USE IT FOR HAIR, BODY OR BLING
—TRY IT FOR EVERYTHING!

By Jean Olsen, BA, LMT, CNMT, HEFT

Original edition published by
Abundance Enterprises, Inc., Sarasota, FL 34234 USA

Digital edition published October 2014 by
Suncoast Digital Press, Inc., Sarasota, FL, 34234 USA

ISBN 978-1-939237-33-0

Start adding coconut oil into your diet.

Check out my tasty *20 Delicious Coconut Oil Recipes*
free on my web site at:
http://jeanolsen.com

CONTENTS

DEDICATION

This book is dedicated to Karen and Wayne Potter. They are wonderful clients/friends of mine who first told me about coconut oil. When they first greeted me at their door they had a covered dish of the oil. "We can't believe you haven't heard about this stuff," they said to me. "It's great!" There is a possibility that I had been told about coconut oil before this, but their exuberance made me pay attention this time.

They are mindful, health-conscious people who are always striving to do the right things, avoid chemicals, and help the environment. Had it not been for their enthusiasm and knowledge about coconut oil, I might never have learned about it.

Also, I would like to give thanks to all my patients and friends who have supported me over the years. A number of you have contributed your experiences with using coconut oil, and I have hopefully included all of you here. Your kindness and encouragement have made my life more focused, inspired and dedicated. Without you, I would not have completed this book. Thank you!

INTRODUCTION

About two years ago, I got a call from a couple to come to their office to perform my "workplace massage" service, one of the various ways I help clients in my Licensed Massage Therapy business. When I asked how they had heard about me, I wasn't surprised to learn that they were referred by my client, who is a chiropractor and often recommends my massage services.

When I go to someone's home or office, I bring all my equipment with me—my massage table, a bolster, sheets, a foam cushion, a portable stereo, and my massage oils. But these new clients, Karen and Wayne, told me on the phone that I did not need to bother bringing any oil; they had some there. This was a little disconcerting because of prior situations where people had their own oils that were not as good as the oils I used. But what could I say? Sometimes people had allergies or had found a favorite oil they liked on their skin, so I was ready to go along with what they wanted to use. What I wasn't prepared for was that Karen and Wayne were going to change my life forever.

This was how I was first introduced to coconut oil. They told me they loved it because of all of its health and beauty benefits. They had been experimenting with all the applications of coconut oil, such as a moisturizing their skin and conditioning their hair. They also loved the taste of it and put it on many things, and especially liked it on their toast in the morning.

There was a little bowl of it up on the counter and they told me about how the consistency of it would change depending on the temperature. Though thermostats can vary, the point at which it changes from a solid to a liquid is around 74-76 degrees. When I put it in my warm hands, it softened, responding almost instantly to my touch. This made it especially intriguing.

The type of massage I do is a combination of Swedish and neuromuscular, which requires that the oil or lotion that I use is the right consistency. The Swedish massage process demands that the oil helps my hands to glide across the skin. The neuromuscular aspect means that what I use must be able to help me to grip, as well, without losing a firm connection with someone's skin or musculature. I was impressed that coconut oil was perfect for my massage, as my hand work felt smooth yet firm with the use of it. By the time I completed the massages for Karen and Wayne, I had a keen appreciation for their wonderful coconut oil.

Since then, I have been doing my own experiments and research on the various uses of coconut oil. I went through a phase where I was trying it on or with everything. In this book I lovingly refer to this as my TIFE (Try It For Everything) stage.

Coconut oil is a wildly versatile oil, as you will read about. Some of what I found out really surprised me, as I'm sure it will you, too. I've included some interesting and valid information about the health benefits I discovered in my research. Also, to help you get started with your own ideas for incorporating coconut oil into your life, I will share with you many of my tried-and-true original recipes.

It is my hope that you will enjoy learning about the many uses of this unique and wonderful oil. As you begin to try it, you will be able to stop using many chemically-based products. You will also feel good about your contribution to help resolve our environmental issues, as you won't need to buy, use, or discard toxic chemicals. When you start using coconut oil, you will also be able to clear out some of your cabinets that hold various products, because this oil is so versatile. These reasons alone should encourage you to get started! As your enthusiasm builds, as mine has, you will come up with even more uses of coconut oil on your own. Enjoy!

Chapter 1

ABOUT COCONUT OIL

Coconut oil is an extraction from the meat of mature coconuts, harvested from the coconut palm. It is one of the most beneficial natural products in our world. It is considered by many people to be necessary for good health, as well as for grooming and caring for the body and our environment. It has been used for thousands of years by native island cultures and is an integral part of daily life for many people living today in tropical or subtropical areas of the world.

In our culture, the use of coconut oil requires that we break out of some social conditioning that influences us to use highly-marketed chemical products. We also need to be conscious of the (undeserved) bad rap that coconut oil has gotten in the past and continues to suffer today.

There are so many benefits to using coconut oil, both for ourselves and for our environment. My research led me to information about using coconut oil in treating everything from HIV to insomnia. It is capable of reducing the effects of aging, thanks to its power as an emollient and an antioxidant. What I have also discovered is that there are multiple ways of incorporating coconut oil into your environment and reducing the negative impact of chemicals.

Some people question the health benefits of coconut oil because it is a saturated fat. The truth about saturated fats is that there are many different types of them, some good and some bad. Because coconut oil is taken from a plant source, it is very different from the saturated oils taken from an animal product.

There are ten different medium chain fatty acids (MCFA) in coconut oil. Lauric acid is by far the most prevalent. This MCFA, which is also abundantly present in human breast milk, provides the building blocks of growth and good health. In addition, it is known for its antimicrobial benefits, which support a healthy immune system. Its presence is a large part of what makes coconut oil especially healthy for us.

Many health concerns can be helped with coconut oil, either directly or indirectly. For instance, it is helpful for weight loss by improving one's metabolism and bolstering the thyroid gland's good health. .With obesity comes a myriad of other problems including varicose veins, high blood pressure, heart issues, knee and foot pain, digestive disturbances, depression—just to name a few. As part of healthy eating and an active lifestyle, coconut oil is a essential food to keep on hand to obtain and maintain a healthy body weight and body fat percentage.

Coconut oil is widely considered to be an antiviral, antifungal, antibacterial, antimicrobial and antiprotozoal food. Some of these terms are easy enough to understand: antiviral (kills viruses), antibacterial (kills bacteria), antifungal (kills fungus), and antimicrobial (kills algae, fungi, bacteria and parasites). However, before my research I didn't know what "antiprotozoal" meant. Do you? This means that it kills protozoa, which is a single-celled organism and parasite. It typically causes infections such as malaria, giardiasis and trichomoniasis. The fact that coconut oil can fight off these diseases definitely speaks to its health benefits!

When we invite coconut oil into our routine, we are making a paradigm shift in our lifestyles. For instance, we no longer need to go to the dentist to have our teeth cleaned as often. The oil helps our body to absorb minerals such as calcium and magnesium which encourages the strength of our teeth, particularly the enamel. With all its antimicrobial and antioxidant benefits, it is no wonder that it keeps our gums healthy, as well. Even though it seems to be a time-consuming venture to change our ways, in actuality, the use of coconut oil carves out more time for us. In the instance above, how much time do you set aside for dental appointments and how many hours do you need to work to pay for those appointments?

A lot of things that we use, especially in lubricants, paint, carpets, building materials insulation, and plywood, have high levels of VOCs (volatile organic compounds), which are detrimental to us. Not only do our bodies absorb these compounds when we use them, but they also vaporize to a breathable gas. Manufacturing and disposing of them produces hazardous waste that pollutes our air and water. Typically, coconut oil can replace these products with no harmful effects to our environment or our bodies.

Coconut oil has gotten a bad reputation in the past. From what I read, it seems as if some of the bad rap has a political/economic basis to it. For instance, we were told years ago that fat was bad for us, especially saturated fats, but now we are finding that it just isn't the truth. This book will not center on this debate, as my intent is simply to expose you to all the wonderful, healthy ways to use coconut oil. This is just a fair warning that you might come across misinformation that will steer you away from coconut oil.

In this book, I won't go deeply into the chemistry of coconut oil, nor will I delve into the history of it. This book is about using coconut oil, so I will leave these topics for other books. I have provided a list of references and research sources at the back of this book; if you are curious to learn more about this topic.

Chapter 2

USING COCONUT OIL IN THE HOME

A lot of the ways I perfected the use of coconut oil in the home was through inspiration, then trial and error. There were times when I would question my sanity because I was spending every waking hour thinking about the use of coconut oil. But most of the ideas really worked, so I was happy that I stayed open-minded. These were what I considered the Try It for Everything (TIFE) days.

When you replace the chemicals in your home with a natural, healthy product, you are contributing to a healthier home. And if we all used fewer chemicals, think of how that would cut back on our carbon footprint. Considering also the simplicity of working with coconut oil and its numerous healing benefits, it is a worthy addition to any household.

Hopefully, while browsing through and trying out these applications, you will come up with even more uses for coconut oil. If you do, please share them with me—if you come across a great coconut oil discovery and bring it to my attention, I will gladly give you credit for the find in a future work.

USE #1   REVITALIZES LEATHER

Okay, so I'm a lax person who lets her dogs up on the furniture—but I uncovered another use of coconut oil because of it!

One of my dogs had clambered up on my leather couch and his nails had scratched the surface. This was, thankfully, during my TIFE days, so I didn't hesitate to bring out my coconut oil. I took a clean paper towel and dipped it into the oil. Then, I began rubbing it into the spot that was scratched.

Not only did it almost completely hide the scratched area, but it also made the area look clean and conditioned. So, I continued polishing the whole couch with the oil. Before I let anyone sit on it, I left it alone for a couple of hours. Then I went back and took a soft cloth and polished some more. It was like my couch had undergone a face lift and looked years younger!

I'm sure you could use this on any kind of leather product, like a purse or shoes. To get the full benefits, just make sure you let it sink in for a while and then go back and thoroughly rub any residue or oily areas.

USE #2   POLISHES FURNITURE

This is another one of those TIFE experiences that occurred after I saw how well it conditioned my leather furniture. In fact, I still had coconut oil in my hand and had some left on the paper towel I had used to put it on the leather couch. So, I decided to try it on a wooden table I had sitting next to the couch. Not only did it loosen some dirt in the corners, but it dusted it and polished it up all in one swoop!

One downside of using this method is that furniture polished with coconut oil seems to lose its shine slightly faster than it would with chemical polish. However, I believe the eco-friendly nature of coconut oil approach more than makes up for this issue.

USE #3   LUBRICATES KEYHOLES

This one will blow you away. First, some context: my front door is temperamental. If I don't spray WD-40 in the keyhole every six months or so, it becomes difficult to open. I have no idea why, nor does anyone else I ask. This last time it got stuck, I decided to try coconut oil on it instead. I put a little on the key itself and inserted it, wiggled it around a little and guess what? It opened—no problem.

If you decide to try this method, I do have one word of caution. I haven't personally seen any harmful long-term effects of using coconut oil in my keyhole, but I live in Florida, and I suspect that someone in a colder climate might see the oil residue build up and congeal over time. If you're concerned about such a risk, I recommend applying as little oil as possible to the key, and only using this method once or twice a year.

USE #4   CONDITIONS PLANT LEAVES

The "elephant ear" plants that I have look really good when they are shiny. It makes them look vibrant and healthier and as if I am paying attention to every little detail of my housekeeping. So, I put a little coconut oil on a soft cloth and shine them up with it. As with most of the uses described in this chapter, a little goes a long way. So far, all of my plants have responded beautifully to this treatment, but if you have a particularly fragile or vulnerable variety in your home, I recommend doing some additional research before trying this method on it.

USE #5   CLEANS MARBLE TOPS

My parents passed on to me a beautiful piece of furniture from Germany. It is a type of hutch that is wooden on the bottom with a marble top. Again, I was in a TIFE mood, so I took a lint-free cloth and dipped it into coconut oil. It cleaned off any dust that was there and it left a gorgeous shine. This made the furniture look even more expensive and well cared for. I am not sure how well it sinks into marble but it certainly seemed to condition it. My parents would be proud!

USE #6   PUTS THE TWINKLE BACK IN CANDLES

You know how big candles that have been sitting out on display start to look drab? I was sitting in my living room one day looking at how lackluster some things looked, and these caught my eye in particular. It was in the TIFE days, so, I got up and got a cloth, dipped it into coconut oil and began using it to shine the outer parts of my large, decorative candles. It worked much better than my prior methods—dust sticks to candles and can't just be swished off, and a damp cloth removed dust but still left the candles dull and drab. Not this time!

This takes very little effort and oil, and the result is a much brighter, cleaner bit of decor. Also, since it is an oil and not a chemical, it will not interfere with the burning process or pollute the air in your home.

USE #7   CREATES MORE GLITTER IN YOUR JEWELRY

Rings, bracelets, watch bands, beads, earrings—the more they are worn, the more worn they look, and we've all tried various chemicals to restore the bling to our bling. The great news is that nature's own coconut oil can be used to polish practically anything, big or small. The other day, for instance,

I took my emerald and diamond ring and let it sit in the oil for a few hours. Then I took it out and wiped it with a dry paper towel. The gold band cleaned up nicely but otherwise didn't show much change, but the stones were really shiny and still sparkled even after many days of normal wear, hand-washing, and so forth.

You probably wear most of your rings and other good jewelry on a daily basis, don't you? Every jewelry cleaner that I have seen has harsh chemicals in it. Now, I know it's not a lot but when you constantly have chemicals touching your skin and seeping in around your neck or your fingers, it can't be good for you. When you can, why not be on the safe side? Coconut oil may not take the tarnish off of a metal, but it will certainly shine it up.

USE #8   SPIFFIES UP CABINETS

My cabinets are, unfortunately, made out of veneer. I wish they were made of real wood, but I made this decision years ago and just have to live with it. To make the best of it, I try to keep them looking spiffy. The other day I took a cloth with some coconut oil on it and rubbed it all over them. It made them look brand new, and almost like real wood! The ease and cost-effectiveness of this method actually made me glad for once that I'd settled on the veneer.

USE #9   SHINES UP THE BACKSPLASH

When I redid my kitchen I spent more money on the backsplash than just about anything! I just fell in love with this particular tile. When I was in a TIFE mood I went ahead and put a little of coconut oil on the backsplash and it shined it up. It looks beautiful and just like it did when I first had it put up. Even the backsplash in my RV, which is made of a lightweight aluminum, looked considerably better after a very light application of coconut oil.

USE #10 CLEANS/SHINES TUB AND FIXTURES

This use seemed crazy at first, but today it is one of my favorites. It is one I use all the time.

I have a Jacuzzi in my one bathroom that I just love to soak in. After a while, a huge ring of dirt forms. Usually it is a big hassle for me to bend over and clean this huge tub with a disinfectant powder cleanser. What made it even harder is I try and hold my breath the whole time as I can tell that breathing the cleanser fumes is toxic. One day, I took some coconut oil on a wash cloth and began scrubbing. I thought I would need to add salt or some sort of abrasive, but it cleaned right off on its own.

Then I got carried away and began using it on all the fixtures in the bathroom. My bathroom sparkled! The real beauty is that I also don't have to be concerned about having chemicals near my body when I am in the bathroom.

Here's another added benefit to this that even I couldn't believe at first. After you have used the oil on your tub, the next time you take a bath, the scum doesn't stay. It's as if you almost don't have to clean it. Can you believe it? It's like a non-stick skillet. Is anyone out there reading this as excited as me or am I just nuts? I imagine that it is because the scum slides off the oily surface that you don't see any dirt on it afterwards. When I take a soak in the tub I am using really hot water, too which makes it even more interesting that it doesn't need to be cleaned the next time.

The next time, just to challenge myself, I left the scum on for a few days. I wanted to see how easy it would be to get it off after it had time to really stick. I took a cloth that was a little damp and put coconut oil on it. It was so easy to get off, I just couldn't believe it. The oil worked so thoroughly and effortlessly, and without the help of a single unhealthy chemical compound!

USE #11   CONDITIONS/CLEANS/SHINES YOUR CAR, BIKE, TRUCK, RV

You are going to love this one when you see the results of what coconut oil can do here—I'm definitely proud of this discovery. It truly will blow your mind.

I have a Honda Element, which has an interior that is mostly vinyl with some leather. The exterior also has a lot of vinyl on it. Every once in a while I will clean the inside and try to make it shiny, but I dislike the use of chemicals. So, you guessed it—I used coconut oil on the inside of my car.

I dipped the cloth into the oil and then rubbed it in. In a few minutes I knew I was on to something here, because it started looking beautiful. The first place I put it was on the dashboard, then I got brave and began going around all the gadgets in the front. The most dramatic effect occurred after I used it on the steering wheel. It looked brand new! I know from my experience with furniture that the oil will work just as wonderfully with any vehicle's leather interior—the only instance where I would not recommend using it is, of course, on cloth.

Then I began rubbing it into the outside of the car, as well. As I said, there is a lot of vinyl on the exterior so I began rubbing it on there with very little pressure. Again, I bravely began wiping it on the whole outside of the car! It looked so shiny and the dirt came off on the rag so I didn't have to go through the whole mess of water cleanup. When I showed my friends and family, they couldn't believe it!

My mechanic, David DeSisto of Car Tuneup (www.cartuneup.net) here in Sarasota, Florida, says that you never want to use a petroleum-based product on the inside of your car. This is because, over time, as the sun shines through the windshields they amplify the heat. The heat burns the petroleum product and it will eventually deteriorate whatever you're putting it on. Dashboards, steering wheels, etc. are especially prone to deterioration due to the constant exposure to the sun. We know this in Florida!

"If you can, start using coconut oil when the car is new," David advises. "This is because once it has started to deteriorate, it is more difficult to get its liveliness back." The first time I used the oil with my car it didn't have as beautiful of an outcome as the second time. And the next time it not only absorbed better, it also stayed looking shiny for a longer time.

Anything Dave says I listen to because he has been my mechanic for over 30 years and has never steered me wrong. It's interesting how even car mechanics are now recognizing the adverse effects of petroleum-based products, isn't it?

Chapter 3

COCONUT OIL AND HEALTH

There are so many health benefits associated with using coconut oil that it would be impossible to cover them all. Because of its unique properties of being antimicrobial, antibacterial, antifungal and antiprotozoal, the health uses are just about limitless. It is also a powerful antioxidant, meaning it reduces inflammation in the body, which is a major contributor to many diseases.

Every day I ingest at least two tablespoons of coconut oil. I do this for a myriad of reasons but mostly because my holistic MD, Dr. Monhollon (www.floridaintegrative.com) advocates the use of it. He uses Applied Kinesiology (muscle strength testing) to help determine how much I personally need. The last time I went to see him, I told him I was writing this book and asked for any suggestions to give my readers. He said that most people could benefit from at least one tablespoon per day.

Dr. Monhollon also said that his father has signs of dementia, and he has recommended that he ingest the oil. He has him taking seven tablespoons of coconut oil per day. Obviously, he believes in the healing powers of coconut oil.

There is so much information written about the healing powers of coconut oil. Just when I think I know everything there is about the oil, I find out more. Based on what I read and what others have told me, I have compiled this list. It includes things that I have tried it for, people around me have told me about, and uses I discovered in my research.

I am confident you will find something in this list that you can put to use for yourself or your loved ones.

DISCLAIMER: None of the information here is intended to take the place of medical advice, diagnosis or treatment. For serious health questions or concerns, please consult your physician.

USE #12   HEALS FUNGAL INFECTIONS ON TOES AND FEET

Fortunately, I have never gotten a fungal itch between my toes or on my feet. I have heard it can be quite distracting. One of the properties of coconut oil is that it is antifungal. Because of this, I know it could replace the use of chemicals in treating fungal infections on the toes or, really, anywhere. I totally support the use of non-chemicals for a myriad of reasons, in treating anything.

The success stories I've read recommend that if you have a fungal infection on your toes, apply the oil every night before going to bed and put some cotton socks on. Because you can't use too much coconut oil, especially with this sort of problem, it is safe to say you could try this remedy every night until the fungal problem was solved.

USE #13   SOOTHES HEMORROIDS

Okay, I know this is not the most pleasant topic. However, if you've ever had hemorrhoids, you will be grateful for this remedy.

As a massage therapist, many patients tell me their secrets. Some of the secrets I often get to hear about are the challenges they are too embarrassed to tell other people. Lucky me!.

Recently, someone told me about her hemorrhoid problem and I suggested she try coconut oil for the following reasons: When you put the oil on the affected area, it brings down swelling because of its anti-inflammatory properties. It can also be helpful to apply the oil a little further up into the rectum to relieve inflamed areas and to provide lubrication so there is no stress and strain during a bowel movement.

There is another way coconut oil, when ingested, will help with hemorrhoids. Instead of just treating them, why not do what we can to prevent them from occurring? When our digestive system is poor we are more apt to get hemorrhoids from any straining because of constipation. The oil helps with our digestion, which heals constipation. I can attest to this.

USE #14   ALLEVIATES BUMPS ON THE TONGUE

Do you ever get those little raised bumps on your tongue? I do. Actually, the bumps on our tongues are nodules called papillae, which can become inflamed. Usually, this inflammation is nothing to be concerned about, especially if they go away after a day or two. Sometimes, though, this can indicate a more serious condition such as a vitamin deficiency, some form of oral cancer, or even an auto-immune deficiency such as AIDS. If you have this problem a lot, it is important to have it checked out with your doctor. But, if not, you can benefit from reading about my experience with them and coconut oil.

I've tried a lot of things to heal these bumps, including everything that's written about nutritional deficiencies. Since adhering to some of the nutritional advice I've read about I get them less often, but I still get them. The last few times they

15

popped up, I took a tablespoon of coconut oil and swished it around in my mouth for about 15 minutes. Then I spit it out.

Most of the time, these little bumps hang around for at least a couple of days. When I did the 15 minute swishing, they were gone in less than 24 hours. It's probably because of the anti-inflammatory properties of the oil that squelched them. It could also be because the problem has a viral component and the oil is antiviral, as well. Maybe it is a combination of the two; it is difficult to say. The bottom line, though, is that, even if it doesn't help you as much as it helped me, it's safe enough that it won't hurt to try.

USE #15   GETS RID OF CANKER SORES

Sometimes I get those mouth sores that may be brought on by stress, acidity, or some other type of disturbance to my system. I have not been able to figure out exactly what brings them on. Maybe someday I will figure it out, but in the meantime I have found a solution to getting rid of them much more quickly than before. They used to take days to clear up. Today, what I do is put some coconut oil in my mouth and swish it around for at least 15 minutes.

While doing this, I make sure to expose any particularly pained areas to an extra amount of oil. I do this because it seems to soothe the painful irritation for me. It must be the antifungal and/or the antiviral properties of coconut oil, but whatever the magic is, within 24 hours the sores are always gone.

USE #16   RAISES METABOLISM

When our metabolism is functioning optimally, our bodies are more able to perform a myriad of beneficial jobs.

This includes everything from digesting our foods to absorbing them better, repairing damaged organs, and generally giving us more stamina.

About 30 years ago I was diagnosed with hypothyroidism, so when I heard that coconut oil improves one's thyroid function, I was very interested in learning more. For about six months now, as of the writing of this book, I have been taking about two tablespoons per day. My last blood test revealed that my thyroid is in a normal range, though I am also taking Armour thryroid, so this is a difficult one for me to assess for myself. Since I did read of many instances where people report the oil has helped to heal the thyroid, I will continue to do this one simple practice which has no downside and could be helping me in this very important health issue.

USE #17   CREATES MORE ENERGY

When I began taking the oil months ago, I didn't notice a difference at first in my energy level. Today, though, I am sure coconut oil is increasing my energy levels. It provides a nice, long energy boost, unlike some things that just jazz you up for an hour or two. It is more subtle and long lasting. I also find I need less sleep and wake up feeling refreshed more often, thanks to my daily oil intake.

USE #18   INCREASES HEART HEALTH

There are many possible contributions to heart disease. Ingesting coconut oil addresses most of the ones that I have read about. Because of its power as an antioxidant, it neutralizes free radicals which can cause inflammation that may lead to heart disease. Coconut oil protects the heart and arteries from bacteria and viruses. Our blood's ability to become too sticky and therefore create buildup in the arteries is lessened with regular use of coconut oil. There is a known relationship between gum disease and poor heart health that is helped with regular use of this magnificent oil.

We have been trained to believe that all saturated fats are bad for the heart. When you really study the attributes of coconut oil and how it breaks down in the body, you will know what false information we have been given. If this is an area of concern for you I highly recommend reading "The Coconut Oil Miracle" by Bruce Fife, C.N., N.D.

USE #19   AIDS DIGESTION

I can't say for sure how it is helping me, but my digestion is much better than it used to be before I began my daily practice of taking coconut oil. As I said earlier, I currently take at least two tablespoons of the oil per day. There are many reasons why I may have had digestion problems. For one thing, I don't handle stress that well, I have an underactive thyroid, and I have a bad habit of eating too fast. These are all contributors to digestive problems including poor absorption of nutrients, constipation, and bloating.

Today, I still have all of these contributors and yet my digestion is so much better. Is it because the oil has improved my hypothyroidism, which can be one of the factors? Who knows? I just know that it has improved since I started ingesting the oil on a daily basis.

USE #20   SUPPORTS WEIGHT LOSS

Another thing that people experience with regular use of coconut oil is weight loss. There are a lot of articles to support this, especially on the internet. Despite the fact that I have hypothyroidism, my weight has remained fairly constant since I started taking coconut oil daily. Actually, I have been eating more than usual lately, and still haven't had any weight gain.

When people report weight loss from ingesting coconut oil it could be because of a couple reasons. One of these is that it increases metabolism, either by a direct or indirect result of healing the thyroid. Another reason is that when you ingest coconut oil, there is a certain satiating effect that takes place. Feeling less hungry results in less of a desire to overeat. Still another reason could be the interplay between hormonal healing that takes place when ingesting the oil. When all of our hormones are in balance, there is more of a tendency to maintain our normal weight. Another benefit of coconut oil that may play a part in weight loss is that it balances blood sugar levels. When our sugar levels are not spiking, there is less of a tendency to overeat and/or crave sweets. One more reason that I believe may play a role in weight loss is that coconut oil reduces inflammation in the body. A reduction of inflammation helps to create a better atmosphere in the body for proper absorption of food, a more optimal metabolism, and weight loss. And, of course, it could be a combination of all of these reasons.

USE #21   INCREASES SEXUAL PLEASURE

Don't worry, "Jane," I won't put your real name in this part of the book as the person who told me about using coconut oil as a sexual lubricant. But you did tell me about how it helped keep things soft and moist. You also told me it helps to heal any type of irritation to the skin.

Also, because of its great scent and taste, you can use it for all kinds of sexual play. And no, I have not personally experienced this yet, but I believe the person who told me! She said it feels very natural and she is happy to put it in her body, as opposed to commercial brands of lubricant.

USE #22   BOOSTS THE IMMUNE SYSTEM

If you search for the benefits of coconut oil, you are sure to come up with much information about the immune-system-boosting aspects of this miraculous oil. In fact, this is a huge reason why a lot of people take it. There is documented research on groups of people, such as AIDS patients, who are benefiting from some of what coconut oil can do in this area. In the book "The Coconut Oil Miracle" by Bruce Fife, C.N., N.D., he writes about the germ-fighting benefits of the oil and outlines some of the clinical studies, especially with AIDS patients.

There are a multitude of reasons why coconut oil is an immunity booster. Once again, it is probably the anti-inflammatory benefits of the oil that create such a supportive environment for healing. Also, some of the benefits of the medium chain fatty acids play a role in immunity boosting. Coconut oil also increases the body's ability to absorb nutrients, which, of course, will help with immunity. Another contributing factor is the high levels of antioxidants that support a healthy immune system.

USE #23   BALANCES HORMONE LEVELS

Most people need additional nutritional support for the balanced health of their hormones. If we do not have our hormones in balance and doing their job, our bodies will suffer. This is mainly because our hormones are, essentially, our bodies' messengers. Basically they affect many aspects of your health by traveling in your bloodstream throughout your whole body, bringing information to various organs.

Coconut oil is wonderful for hormone health. Our hormones need healthy fats in order to continue keeping them at optimal health. The medium chain fatty acids that are in coconut oil are fundamental to hormone production.

For most of my life I have struggled with hypothyroidism and weak adrenal glands. Since ingesting the oil on a daily basis for over six months now, I can say that I do feel more energy. This is usually indicative of the thyroid starting to heal and the adrenal glands being more able to handle stress without becoming fatigued. Wouldn't that be nice if it were as simple as ingesting coconut oil?

Hormonal balances change in both men and women as they age. Women tell me that coconut oil seems to help with symptoms associated with menopause.

USE #24   LEVELS BLOOD SUGAR ISSUES

Because I am slightly hypoglycemic, I am always trying to be aware of how and when my sugar levels spike. Since I started taking coconut oil on a daily basis, I do not crave sugary goodies as much. I believe it is because of the daily use of coconut oil that this is happening. As mentioned in other use examples, coconut oil can make you feel less hungry— what we call hunger pains are often symptoms caused by a drop in blood sugar levels. If we eat a carbohydrate snack, the relief is very temporary and the body's insulin response can actually cause us to feel more out of balance. Have you ever had the sugar high followed by the sugar crash? Ingesting coconut oil will never cause that to happen.

If you suffer from problems with your blood sugar levels, taking coconut oil daily may be an option for you. You may want to check with your doctor first, though, as you never want a condition like diabetes to go undiagnosed.

USE #25   IMPROVES BONE STRENGTH

This is not one use that I have personally experienced; however, I have read a lot about coconut oil's ability to strengthen the bones. When I started researching why bone strength is increased with the ingestion of coconut oil I came up with an interesting explanation. One thing that happens when you take the oil is that your ability to absorb nutrients is increased. Two of these beneficial substances are calcium and magnesium. We all know that these two minerals will promote healthy bones and stave off both osteoarthritis and osteoporosis.

As I've said, this is one health use of coconut oil that I have no personal experience with. I have included it because one of the reasons I am ingesting the oil is that I am hopeful that it will help me in this particular area, among others. There is a history of brittle bones in my family and it is a concern for me. It is one of the uses that I have only read about but, I figure, once again, if it doesn't help, it won't hurt.

USE #26   DECREASES CANDIDA

Candida is a fungus that, in small amounts and in the right places (that is, the intestines and stomach), it is harmless to a person. An overabundance, though, can create all kinds of problems. It can lead to conditions such as vaginal infections, jock itch, athlete's foot and thrush. There are many reasons why we get an overabundance of candida in our system, but probably the two biggest reasons are taking antibiotics and eating too much sugar.

There are a number of reasons why coconut oil addresses candida in the body. For one thing, it is highly antifungal, thanks to its abundance of caprylic, capric and lauric acid. There are two other main reasons why ingesting coconut oil can be helpful when dealing with a candida overgrowth. One reason is it can enhance the body's immune system, which makes one less prone to yeast infections. Another reason why coconut oil is helpful in treating candida is that it naturally satisfies your sweet tooth. It can take the place of many harmful sugars, which can create unhealthy flora in the gut.

If you are a long time sufferer of candida or are having multiple symptoms from candida, probably the best thing you could do would be to go on a coconut oil cleanse. One of my patients did this by first adding a tablespoon per day to her diet. Then she began fasting with just vegetable juice for a few days at a time. She did this off and on for months.

Gradually, she added more coconut oil, and if she started feeling queasy or had diarrhea, she backed off on her dosage. She also tried taking it over the course of the day rather than all at once. Last time we talked about it, she was taking about four tablespoons a day. Because she was having chronic vaginal infections, she put some of the oil on a tampon at night and slept with it in. After her cleansing reactions, she felt really good and some of her other physical complaints, (that she didn't know were part of the candida overgrowth), also subsided. This included digestive problems, especially.

Here is a warning about taking coconut oil for candida overgrowth. If you detox too much at once you may have some problems. Coconut oil is an antimicrobial which helps in cleaning up any microbes that may stick around after killing off a lot of candida but still, it might be too much for your system. If you are feeling overly nauseous, fatigued or achy, simply cut back on your dosage. Of course, if you have any other serious medical conditions that you are seeing a doctor for, please consult with them beforehand.

USE #27   ALLEVIATES THROAT INFECTIONS

If you suspect a cold coming on and your throat feels sore, take about one tablespoon of coconut oil and alternate gargling and swishing in the mouth with it. Do this for at least ten minutes. If your throat soreness has to do with an antibacterial infection or is due to inflammation, this trick will help to ease it. If you have a cold coming on coconut oil helps to fight infection of any kind and is also good for boosting your immune abilities.

USE #28   EASES EAR INFECTIONS

My patients tell me all kinds of stories about their health challenges and often they share the remedies they've discovered as well. One of my patients told me she had chronic ear infections until she started using coconut oil. She began putting the liquefied oil in a dropper and put just two drops in her ear. She did this before she went to sleep at night, so she would turn her head so that the affected side would be up and the oil would drain down deep into the ear.

Before beginning this routine, of course, she had checked with her doctor. She wanted to make sure there wasn't an obstruction or that there wasn't something wrong with the ear other than an infection. Once she knew it wasn't something worse, she could let the anti inflammatory qualities of coconut oil help heal her condition.

USE #29   IMPROVES MEMORY

Wow! There is so much information of the use of coconut oil for memory improvement. As I've said earlier, I ingest at least two tablespoons of coconut oil per day. There are lots of reasons why I take it but one of the biggest reasons is because I am hoping my memory will get better and better. Many people report that, after regular use of coconut oil, they definitely recognize that their memory has improved.

After taking the oil daily for a couple of months now, I definitely do feel like my memory is improving. It seems as if my thinking has generally improved; I am more able to focus and follow through on an idea. I can't say for sure whether this is because of the coconut oil, but considering all the other good things this routine has brought to my health, I look forward to having my memory and cognition improve even more. Wouldn't you like this for yourself and your loved ones?

USE #30   RELIEVES CONSTIPATION

This is one that I can personally attest to. As I've said, I have been ingesting at least two tablespoons of coconut oil for months now with all kinds of remarkable results. It is a natural home remedy that really works for me. In fact, I have never had anything work so well for me for moving my bowels.

It is not completely clear cut as to what creates a healthier situation. From what I have read, it is most likely the medium chain fatty acids (MCFAs) in coconut oil that encourage bowel movement. This is because they are a natural stool softener. However, I believe that when our metabolism is increased, as coconut oil encourages, that that can help to alleviate constipation, as well.

Every person is different, so how much you need will be different from how much someone else will need. It probably depends mostly on two factors. They are how your body reacts to MCFAs and how serious your constipation is. You can always start out taking less than one tablespoon and increasing it gradually. You could also try taking some in the morning and then some in the evening. If you take too much you will get diarrhea, so just lessen the amount until you don't have it any more. Your body may take some time to adjust, so you can always go back and add more of the oil and see how you do.

USE #31   SOOTHES JOCK ITCH

Obviously, since I am female, I have never gotten jock itch. But I did ask a certain male (who wishes to remain anonymous) about using coconut oil for this. He told me it alleviates the burning, itchy feeling and even brings down the redness associated with it. It makes sense that it would, because it is antifungal. Its anti-inflammatory abilities will immediately stop the discomfort associated with jock itch.

You may not need to continue applying the oil for this condition for very long. From what I've read and heard from those using this remedy, usually four days of application will clear it up. This is, of course, if you keep the area dry, so the fungus or bacteria does not continue to have an ideal environment in which to grow.

If the above method doesn't clear up the problem, you may need more of an internal cleansing, especially if you have recurring jock itch.

USE#32   REDUCES STITCHES COMPLICATIONS

Personally I have not had any stitches, but the idea that coconut oil would help with them makes sense. Given all of the beneficial properties of coconut oil, it is no wonder that it would be good for quicker healing when it comes to stitches. Reducing inflammation, softening the skin, and warding off bacteria are all going to contribute to less scarring from stitches.

If I had stitches in I would rub coconut oil over the area every day. This will help reduce future scarring, as well as helping to keep the area soft and bacteria free. Afterwards, I would keep rubbing the oil in, as it will help with healing. Coconut oil is so powerful, and with its high antioxidant levels, it could seep into the area and reduce the time it takes for the skin and underlying area to heal.

USE #33   STRENGTHENS NAILS

I first began researching for this book about six months ago. At that time, I read about the nail-strengthening properties of coconut oil. I read about people whose nails had become stronger after ingesting it and/or putting it on, under, and around their nails.

I had strong nails to begin with, so I didn't notice any changes at first. Today, though, six months later, I've noticed that my nails are even stronger. They are so strong that it is difficult to cut them, and they even grow faster—I have noticed this difference on a daily basis, since, as a massage therapist, I need to keep my nails short.

Although I was not able to find any clear explanation as to why coconut oil is helpful to strengthening nails, it may be because of its ability to help one absorb nutrients. If the body is absorbing nutrients better, the building blocks to all positive developments in the body will be improved, right? I believe that strengthening the nails is similar to strengthening the bones. It is not only about the ingredients in coconut oil, it is about how the oil is a catalyst for our body systems to work more optimally.

USE #34   REDUCES CHOLESTEROL LEVELS

Many people who have sought natural ways to reduce cholesterol levels in their body swear by coconut oil. Replacing your vegetable oils with coconut oil has a positive effect on the body. The medium chain fatty acids (MCFA) in coconut oil, are burned off very rapidly and so, do not affect one's cholesterol levels. Mostly the oil has been shown to have a neutral effect on these levels.

There is a common misunderstanding, even among medical professionals, that the high fat content of coconut oil negatively affects cholesterol levels. Actually, the type of saturated, plant-source fat in this oil has been proven to be totally different than animal-source saturated fat. It is because of this that one can consume coconut oil without cholesterol level concerns.

USE #35   SUPPORTS AFTER-SUN SKIN CARE

When you live in Florida, you need to be aware of any ways to treat sunburn, or even just soothe your skin if you have had just a little too much sun. Many times, I have come home after spending time outdoors with my skin feeling tight and irritated from sun exposure. If I take a little bit of coconut oil and rub it into these areas, I feel immediate relief. One of the things I have yet to try would be to mix coconut oil with aloe vera, but I expect that this would make the oil even more effective.

Coconut oil has a soothing effect that is unsurpassed. It sinks deep into the skin and nourishes it. Also, the anti-inflammatory properties are what bring relief to any overexposed areas. It will also take any redness out of an area. If it seems too greasy for you when you first put it on, wait a little while. If it doesn't sink in, you have put on too much at once, just like when you apply sunscreen. If you use it on a regular basis, your skin will be able to absorb more and more over time.

USE #36   HEALS WITH OIL PULLING

There is a procedure called "oil pulling" that is based on an Ayurvedic practice. (This practice dates back thousands of years and is a holistic approach to wellness and healing, originating in India.) From what I've read, they originally used sesame oil. When you use coconut oil it has even more reported results than if you use sesame oil. There so many health benefits to doing this that I started using it on a daily basis a little while back. Let me first tell you the health benefits and then I will explain this simple procedure.

The benefits reported from this practice are numerous. First of all, it keeps your gums healthy and prevents or heals gingivitis. I've even heard of one person who said they did it a few times a day and it prevented the need for a root canal because it healed the inflammation deep down in their gums. Another reason to do oil pulling is that there are claims that it will whiten your teeth but I have a friend who just wipes down her teeth with the oil and she swears her teeth are whiter. It will also make your breath fresher. Because the oil destroys bacteria, it breaks down plaque. An added benefit that may occur with oil pulling is that is supposedly will help fight cavities. Since this is bringing down inflammation and fighting bacteria in the mouth, it is possible that there are other indirect health benefits that we are not even aware of from oil pulling. Some people claim it also draws metals and other toxins out of the body.

The process is simple: Take about one to two teaspoons and put it in the mouth. Don't take too much because it seems to expand in the mouth as you are doing this. Keep your mouth closed when you are swishing it all around. Make sure you get it in through the teeth and gums and all through the mouth. Do this for about 15-20 minutes. Some people say 15 minutes is enough; others say you need a full 20 minutes, so I'll leave that up to you. When the time is over, spit the oil out. You can do it gently; you don't have to force it to move around. That's it, that's all you do.

This simple procedure could save you lots of aggravation and money in the future. Peridontal disease is very prevalent and easily prevented with this practice. If gingivitis is left untreated it will turn into peridontal disease. If you go into this stage, it means it has gotten worse and there is a significant risk of teeth loss. Now that should make you want to try this!

USE #37   LESSENS HEARTBURN

Supposedly, coconut oil helps with quite a few different digestive disturbances, and heartburn is one of them. Personally, I have not had this experience, but I know a lot of people who have. This is because I haven't had heartburn in years, not since long before I even knew about coconut oil. It makes sense, though, that coconut oil would be helpful with heartburn, since it is so helpful for digestive and absorption issues.

People who report consuming coconut oil to relieve heartburn probably have various ways of using it but one method would be to ingest a tablespoon at the onset of symptoms. Then wait probably about 15 minutes and if it didn't help, I would ingest another tablespoon. You could keep trying this until symptoms subsided. After all, it will not hurt you, if it doesn't help you.

USE #38   PREVENTS TICK BITE PROBLEMS

We know that coconut oil will keep insects off of us. This applies to ticks as well. But, besides keeping them away, coconut oil has another benefit related to ticks. It helps with treating an area that a tick might have bitten.

I go on camping trips a lot with my dogs in my RV. When I went on the last trip, I came back to the RV after hiking with quite a few ticks on me. Some of them were embedded deep in my skin and others hadn't gotten that deep. Of course, when they are embedded in my skin, the first thing I do is pull them straight out with a pair of tweezers. Then the next thing I do is dress the site where the tick was with some coconut oil. Because of its antibacterial properties, it is comforting to do this. Also, it will contribute to the prevention of any scarring that might occur. Since you might not always have a medicinal antibiotic with you, this is a safe alternative.

USE #39   DECREASES BRUISING

One of my dogs pulled me down when we were playing the other day, and I knew I was going to bruise afterwards. I put a little coconut oil on the area and rubbed it in. Of course, it is difficult to say how much I would have bruised, but I feel like it helped diminish some of the coloration. I'm sure it also helped with any sort of inflammation that would have occurred. It is hard to say for sure, but as I usually say: if it doesn't hurt, why not try it?

Chapter 4

COCONUT OIL AND BEAUTY

There are countless ways to use coconut oil for beauty. Wouldn't it be nice to be able to throw away most of what is in your bathroom drawers and cabinets? And wouldn't it feel good to stop using chemicals on your body and in your home? Well, you can with coconut oil.

One of the wonderful things about coconut oil is that it doesn't clog pores, so you can use it to remedy many situations on your skin without worrying about the after-effects. And while you are using it for beauty, it is also healing your skin and hair. That's because it is fighting fungus, bacteria and microbes.

Get ready to change your ways. You will be impressed with the various uses of this wonderful oil. For a while there, every day I was noticing new ways I could use my coconut oil. My hope is that you will also be inspired enough to just begin trying a few of these.

One word of caution: when you are ready to use some oil, do not put your hand or finger into the oil. This will create an unsanitary condition. Instead, pour some into a little container and keep a spoon nearby. When you want to use it, drop the oil from the spoon, rather than touch any oil that is going to go back into your container. The dust, skin cells, dirt or oil on your skin contains bacteria which can grow and contaminate your coconut oil, so it just makes sense to keep it pure. (As a massage therapist, I am always staying aware of any possible unsanitary situations.)

USE #40   CONDITIONS EYEBROWS AND EYELASHES

Supposedly, coconut oil helps to promote hair growth. That means, as you're conditioning your lashes and brows, you may be also increasing their thickness. I have not used coconut oil for an eyelash or eyebrow conditioner on a regular basis yet, but since doing this research I have decided to start!

Try taking a tiny bit of the oil and lubricating your lashes and brows with it. The best time to do this would probably be right before going to sleep. This will let the oil do its work overnight, and you won't have to worry about lingering effects in the morning.

USE #41   EXFOLIATES SKIN

Here's a really money-saving and healthy use of coconut oil. Commercial exfoliants are expensive, and most contain chemicals, as well. Being exposed to chemicals is one thing you never have to worry about when using coconut oil, and the price is definitely reasonable.

Make sure the oil is cooler than 76 degrees so that it is about the consistency of softened butter. Put some coconut oil in a bowl and add an equal amount of sugar to it. Some people like to add salt, too, but others say that will dry out the skin, which defeats the purpose of this project. (Add in coffee grounds to your exfoliant and you will be treating cellulite, as well, according to many holistic practitioners.)

After you are done scrubbing your skin with your exfoliant, rinse the area with warm water. Once it has dried, your skin will be silky soft. Exfoliation removes the oldest, dead skin cells from the surface of your body, thus helping to maintain healthy skin. With coconut oil, the process is more like a spa treat for yourself instead of a chore.

USE #42   MOISTURIZES LIPS

Regular use of coconut oil on your lips will make them moist and supple. Plus, unlike lip gloss and similar products, putting this oil on your lips is good for them. And if you ingest any coconut oil in the process, it will be good for you. Just think of the money you will save, too.

Every once in a while I put coconut oil on my lips. If my lips are dry from sun or salt air, it usually takes a couple of applications. Coconut oil helps my lips feel smooth and sexy. Some people use it every day instead of lipstick because they are concerned about the Food and Drug Administration report that most lipsticks contain toxic metals, or they don't want to use something on their lips which contains rendered animal fat.

USE #43   SHAVES SMOOTHLY AND AVOIDS
RAZOR BURN

Using coconut oil as a shaving lotion is great for a few reasons. For one thing, it nourishes your skin as you're shaving. Also, if you nick yourself or cause razor burn, it will heal while you are shaving. Even if your skin is sensitive, you don't have to purchase shaving lotion for sensitive skin. One time, I was shaving in the shower without coconut oil and I cut too close. I rubbed a tiny bit of the oil on the affected area afterwards and felt immediate relief.

Remember that the oil hardens at a temperature above 76 degrees. If the oil is liquefied, it will apply in a nice thin layer. If it has been kept cool and is somewhat hardened, add a small amount of warm water to it. Apply to the area and shave away.

Here are a couple of warnings. First, be careful when you are using coconut oil in the shower, because it can get slippery. Also, to avoid possible clogging, don't let too much pour down any drain, and let very hot water follow it for twenty seconds.

USE #44   MOISTURIZES BODY/FACE

Using coconut oil on any area of your skin makes it feel soft. It also sinks in, so it will not leave a film, as some moisturizers do. I use it all the time on my face and body and it really feels good. Not only that, but after using it for a while, I've noticed that my skin looks increasingly supple and soft.

Another thing that I've noticed is that the longer I've been using it, the quicker and more thoroughly it sinks in. Now, when I put it on my arms, I look down and the oily look has disappeared. When I first began rubbing it on my skin, it was really shiny for about one to two hours.

When you get out of a bath or shower, your skin needs to have its natural oils replaced. Coconut oil supports the skin's natural ability to replenish itself. It helps the skin avoid infections by establishing the skin's natural antimicrobial barrier. It supports and strengthens the elasticity of your skin. It also helps the body to retain moisture. There are no commercial, all-natural moisturizers that do all of this.

USE #45   CLEANS AS A SOAP OR DETERGENT

If you are so inclined, you can actually make soap out of coconut oil. I have not personally tried to make soap for either washing my body or my clothes, but I wanted to make sure you knew it could be used as a soap. From what I have read, the directions for making soap are similar to making a batch of regular soap. If you go to youtube.com and put in a search for "coconut oil soap" you will see video instructions on how to make detergent from this versatile oil.

USE #46   ERASES UNDER EYE WRINKLES

Here's another product you can quit buying: eye-wrinkle cream. When you apply coconut oil under and around the eyes, you have created a way to diminish fine lines and wrinkles. What you do is, after you have applied the oil as a moisturizer, add a little more around your eyes. If you get some in your eyes by accident, you don't have to worry about it stinging or not being able to get it out of your eye—you can easily rinse it out. In fact, if it gets onto your lashes, it will condition them, too.

USE #47   NOURISHES HAIR AND SCALP

One of the uses of the coconut oil that I was first introduced to, other than as a massage oil, was when Karen told me she used it on her hair as a conditioner. You can now guess correctly that I could not wait to try it!. There are different ways that I use it to condition my hair and scalp.

Try warming the oil and pouring it through your hair. This feels really nice. Then wrap your scalp and hair in a plastic bag and go to sleep. The oil will be working on your hair overnight. Then, of course, wash it out in the morning.

The other way is by just putting it in your hair when it is sitting at less than 76 degrees. This will make it the consistency of butter, so you can just rub it into your hair. You can also put it directly on any especially dry areas, such as the ends. Leave it on for at least an hour if possible. Rinse it out with warm water.

While you are putting coconut oil in your hair as a conditioner, make sure you rub it into the scalp. Not only does this feel really good, but it conditions the scalp, as well. Supposedly, it helps with aiding hair growth by creating a supportive area for hair follicles to replenish.(My friend, Roger, swears it is reversing his baldness!) I also like knowing that if there are any bacteria or icky things going on in my scalp, the oil will be a remedy for those, too.

USE #48   CONTROLS DRY SKIN

If you have chronically dry skin, coconut oil is your answer. Once your body has adapted and is able to absorb it, you can slather it on. This may take a few days but once it does, the healing benefits of coconut oil will improve your condition tremendously. I would not bother using anything else.When you have an especially dry area of skin, use an extra amount there. At first, though, you may have to put it on incrementally. This is because it may take time to sink in. At first it may feel oily, but it will seep into the skin. Most people find that their skin feels wonderful after only a few days of use. Because it is such an all-natural product, it is absorbed easily and it will not create a buildup on the skin.

USE #49   WHITENS TEETH

My friend, Alicia says she uses coconut oil to whiten her teeth. She says she takes a piece of cotton cloth with the oil on it and wipes her teeth. She does this on a daily basis for a few minutes. From what I have read about coconut oil, there are a lot of people who do this on a regular basis. It is so much better for you than the commercial teeth-whitening stuff that is out there. And I've heard that some of those teeth-whiteners can actually strip away the enamel on your teeth. Plus, think of the money you'll save by not buying any of that stuff, and especially by not having to make dental appointments for teeth-whitening.

In Chapter 3, I have included information on "Oil Pulling." This is another way to clean the teeth really well and to whiten them, also. If you don't want to spend the time to do oil pulling and don't need the extra benefit of enhancing the health of your gums, you can just wipe your teeth, as mentioned above. Also, another fan of coconut oil told me she mixes it with baking soda to use as toothpaste and loves the fresher-breath, whiter-teeth results.

USE #50   DEFRIZZES HAIR

If you have curly hair and live in a humid environment, you likely suffer from frizzy hair. Curly hair tends to be dry and wants to soak up the moisture in the air, which causes the hair's cuticles to expand, which therefore causes frizz.

My hair has really changed since I've gotten older. I used to have straight, shiny, thin hair, and now it is wavy, not as shiny, and frizzy, especially in certain areas of my head and in certain weather conditions. I'm not sure what is causing this, probably some kind of hormonal change.

The other day I took a tiny amount of coconut oil and warmed it in the palm of my hand. Then I pressed it into the frizzy areas. My hair relaxed and behaved beautifully after that. If you're going to do this, start out with a very small amount.

What I have found out about coconut oil is that you usually need a whole lot less than you think you do.

USE #51   REMOVES EYE MAKEUP

For years, I have struggled with how to get eye makeup off without the use of chemicals. Some of the things I tried left my eyes feeling oily, and I dealt with vision disturbances because of it. Coconut oil absorbs beautifully into the skin, so after it is used to take off the makeup, the little bit that might remain in the area is simply absorbed into the delicate tissue around the eye to condition it! Not only are you getting your makeup taken off with a healthy means, but you are treating the surrounding areas with this wonderful oil.

USE #52   SOFTENS CUTICLES

Because I do deep neuromuscular work as a massage therapist, I need to be very aware of whether my nails and/or cuticles have the potential to scrape or scratch someone while I am massaging them. It's because of this that I am always trying to soften my cuticles. I found that if I take a tiny amount of coconut oil and just keep pushing it into my cuticle area on a regular basis, it softens the whole area around the nail. Of course, you can use this on your toes, too.

USE #53   MINIMIZES SCARS

When I had acne, I would pick at my facial skin, and that left a few small scars on my face. Since I have been using coconut oil on my face, I do not see them as much anymore. Now I know that most small scars will fade with time, but it seems as if my scars are much less noticeable since using coconut oil. This has taken place in a period of a few months with daily use of applying the oil to my face. Because it is such a pleasant experience (never just an annoying grooming task), I find I use the oil every day without forgetting. I know that scientifically the massaging action of rubbing it into my skin increases circulation to the area which has many side health benefits, and is probably one reason the scars are so much less noticeable.

USE #54   REDUCES STRETCH MARKS

We all have them, don't we? Take a little coconut oil and rub some into areas where you have stretch marks. If you have recently lost or gained a lot of weight, rub it into your skin. If you are planning on gaining or losing weight, begin applying it as soon as possible. The more elasticity your skin has the more easily you can avoid stretch marks, and healthier, moisturized skin has more elasticity.

Another time to think about reducing stretch marks is if you are pregnant, thinking of getting pregnant, or just had a baby. You will be happy you applied coconut oil to help with this.

Chapter 5

COCONUT OIL AND THE KITCHEN

Ingesting coconut oil is not the only reason to have it in the kitchen. In fact, the more places in the kitchen you can find to use the oil, the better. This is because as it is cleaning or shining things up, it is also killing bacteria, fungus, viruses and microbes. Therefore, you are using a nontoxic, chemical-free product that is inexpensive and easy to use. Not only that, but you can cut down on clutter by ditching most of the other products that you are keeping underneath your cabinets.

When you read some of these uses you may wonder if I am nuts—that is, until you try them for yourself. As I've said earlier, when I was in my TIFE (Try It For Everything) days, I came up with all kinds of uses. It was my most creative time for finding out just how versatile the oil is and I was so amazed—well, I had to write a book!

Some of the kitchen uses may surprise you, as they did me. For others, you may wonder why you hadn't thought of them yourself. It is so nice to be able to clean the kitchen area, especially with non-toxic cleaners.

USE #55   MAKES GREAT POPCORN

One night, when I first began using coconut oil I wanted to watch a movie and have some popcorn. There was no canola or olive oil in the house to pop with. I thought "What the heck, I'll try the coconut oil." After all, it's not like I would lose much money trying it if it doesn't work and I had to throw a serving of popcorn out.

For my experiment, I put the same amount that I would if using olive oil and popped as usual. Not only did it work, but I think the popcorn tasted better. It seemed sweeter to me. So I went ahead and put some more of the oil, with salt, on top of the popcorn, as well. The result was so good that this is now the only way I will prepare my popcorn.

For more recipes using coconut oil,
please visit www.jeanolsen.com

USE #56   DAZZLES POTS AND PANS

I have a big, old cast-iron skillet that used to belong to my parents. I've had it for years and it was showing its age, even looking a little rusty in some spots. Many times, I wondered about the best way to keep it in good shape. I'm just not that familiar with this sort of thing, and my parents have both passed. Someone told me about seasoning an iron skillet years ago, so I decided to try using coconut oil on it.

First, I preheated the oven to 250 degrees, and then I used a little sea salt mixed with water to scrub any residue on the skillet. Then, I let the skillet completely dry. My paper towels seemed to be the easiest thing to use, so I dipped one in the oil and rubbed the skillet down really good with a healthy amount of oil. I put the skillet in the oven for about two hours. Then I let it cool. It was that easy. It made the pan shiny, but the oil didn't really sink in so I wiped off the extra oil.

Afterwards, I told a friend I had done this, and she said I should have cured the skillet when it was brand new. This technique ensures a non-stick cooking surface and protects the skillet from rusting. Well, I doubt my parents did this before they gave it to me, because it gets rusty and I need to put oil on it to cook with it.

Then another friend told me she has been using coconut oil to coat her stainless steel pots and pans. She says they look nice and shiny. More importantly, though, this prevents food from sticking the next time you use it. This makes it easier to clean up after cooking.

USE #57   GREASES COOKIE SHEETS

This is an obviously simple use. I was going to bake and bring some cookies to a party, and I didn't know if they would stick to the cookie sheet. So, rather than stress out, wondering if I needed to grease the sheet, I just went ahead and put a thin layer of coconut oil on it before adding the dollops of dough.

The oil made it really easy to remove the cookies when they were done baking. Also, the cookies were not burned on the bottom. Of course, I could have used spray oil or butter, but why not use something that is really healthy for us? I will always have coconut oil on hand for this use.

USE #58   SPIFFS UP COUNTERTOPS

My kitchen cabinets have Corian tops that I pretty much ignore. But one day, when I was in a TIFE mood, I took a paper towel and began polishing up my countertops with coconut oil. Man, did they shine! Plus, when I am using the oil, I am also thoroughly cleaning the surfaces because of the oil's antibacterial and antimicrobial properties.

I am sure it will do the same for other materials, such as granite, marble, Formica and whatever other materials that are being used for countertops today. Like I explained before, you get great results by applying the oil on all the fixtures in the bathroom, so I am sure it will shine up just about anything!

You don't need as much as you would think. Just put a little on a thin rag or even a paper towel and begin rubbing. You will see a difference immediately.

USE #59   POLISHES UTENSILS

My everyday utensils have spots on them. I suppose you'd call them water spots. Also, washing them does not remove all fingerprints. Because of this, my utensils looked dull and dirty—but, thanks to coconut oil, not anymore. When I had a friend over for lunch the other day I just took a little coconut oil on a cloth and wiped them down. I know it may sound silly, but it felt good to do because they looked so much better. But also, I may be cleaning off bacteria, fungus and who knows what when I am cleaning my silverware. I love this stuff!

USE #60   CLEANS CUTTING BOARDS

My client and friend, Susan, says she uses coconut oil on her wooden cutting boards. I missed this one, myself. What a great use for the oil!

She cleans her cutting board as usual. Then, she lets it dry. When it has thoroughly dried, she takes a little coconut oil and rubs it on both sides of her board. This preserves the wood and keeps it looking nice. It also keeps it clean and sterile, because the oil is anti-bacterial and anti-viral— therefore you should use a little on your cutting board even if it is not wooden.

After she told me about her coconut oil find, I decided to try it myself. I have a long, oblong cutting board that I not only use for cutting things up, but I also hang it on my wall for decoration. It looks so much better now. Thanks so much, Susan, for sharing your find with me.

Shortly after this, another client/friend, Diane, told me she uses coconut oil on her plastic cutting board. Sometimes she washes it through the dishwasher and it becomes dull and dry, so she decided to try the oil on it. The process and the results were the same as the wooden cutting board.

Chapter 6

USING IT WITH ESSENTIAL OILS

As a massage therapist, I have taken courses on aromatherapy and have learned to utilize essential oils in my practice. These are not actually oils, but they are distilled, cold-pressed or extracted aroma compounds from natural sources, usually plants. They are used widely for medicinal purposes, or sometimes just for their aroma or flavor. Examples include anise, basil, camphor and lavender. The liquid is so concentrated that it is used in measured drops. When you work with essential oils added into coconut oil, it is helping the effectiveness of the essential oil because coconut oil helps to disperse essential oils throughout the body. When mixing the two, I add a few drops of an essential oil to the liquid form of the coconut oil. When used this way, the coconut oil would be considered the "carrier oil."

Essential oils are from different parts of various plants and have different healing benefits. They have been used for their medicinal qualities since ancient times. The better-quality essential oils are very potent because they are absorbed quickly into the cells. In fact, high quality oils are absorbed by the bloodstream to every cell in the body within minutes.

You can find a lot of essential oils to add to coconut oil either online or in your local health food store. Of course, some are much better for you than others. Less expensive does not always mean lesser quality, but generally speaking, some of the better quality oils are more expensive. Price also greatly varies, simply according to the particular essential oil. For instance, sweet orange is always inexpensive, whereas helichrysum is known to be expensive.

The list below is a compilation of all of the essential oils I have personally used in my practice. I add them to coconut oil for therapeutic purposes. In no way is it a complete list of all the different ways you can use coconut oil with essential oils. There are as many ways to mix coconut oil with essential oils as there are situations in life. So, with a little knowledge you can hopefully start to build an understanding of some of the ways to blend these two types of natural products to create a chemically-free, clean, healthy life and home.

Here are a couple of warnings: If you are pregnant or have major medical problems, please consult with your doctor before using essential oils. If your doctor is not familiar with essential oils please consult with someone in the alternative health field. This is important because, for instance, some essential oils should not be used during pregnancy. One other thing to be aware of is that it is not good to get sun exposure after using some of the essential oils.

Taking care of your essential oils is important, too. Make sure you keep your essential oils out of direct sunlight. Also, cap them after use so they do not lose any of their potency. Keep them in a place where children cannot get to them.

USE #61   APPLIES AS A MASSAGE OIL

Practicing as a licensed massage therapist since 1995, I have tried all kinds of different lotions and potions to massage with. Since being introduced to coconut oil, I don't feel like I need to keep investigating anymore; coconut oil is my absolute favorite. It has so many wonderful qualities and is so good to use for my clients and myself. My inventory is now very simple: one massage oil—coconut.

Here are some other aspects of coconut oil that I like when using it for a massage. For one thing, it never goes rancid. In fact, I've heard of instances of it keeping for years. Also, it is an excellent emollient, which means it effectively softens and moistens any skin it comes in contact with. Unlike many skin creams, it does not cause any buildup on the skin, as it sinks deeply in to regenerate and nourish the skin.

Adding essential oils to coconut oil for massage purposes is fun and will enhance its natural healing abilities. There are so many wonderful varying essential oils. It is impossible to list them all here. Try adding a few drops of your favorite aromatic oil to the coconut oil and rub this on your body. Bring your lovely custom-blend with you the next time you get a massage, and ask your therapist to use it on you.

USE #62   CLEANS YOUR TEETH

Just recently I went on a RV trip. Usually I'm pretty good at remembering what I need, but when I got to the state park I realized I had forgotten my toothpaste. But guess what I did have? My coconut oil and some fennel essential oil.

Now, there are some essential oils that should not be ingested, but since I knew that this particular essential fennel oil was okay (and besides, I was going to spit it out), I decided to go ahead and put a drop on my toothbrush. Then I put a little coconut oil on my brush, too. Now, I know that some people add baking soda to their coconut oil to make toothpaste, and I've even heard of people using salt to create some abrasion to get their teeth really clean. I did not use either of these, but my teeth felt really clean anyway. Maybe the ideal thing to do would be to add some baking soda and/ or salt along with an essential oil and coconut oil. If I had had peppermint essential oil, I would have used that because I like the taste of it better than fennel, but what I had on hand did the job just as well. The other big benefit of using coconut oil to clean your teeth is that is has teeth-whitening power too.

USE #63   PROTECTS AS A SUNSCREEN

After having lived in Florida for more than 30 years, I am very aware of all kinds of sun and surf issues. Native Pacific Islanders have been using coconut oil in many ways, including as a sunscreen. When the oil is applied it provides an SPF (Sun Protection Factor) of 20 as protection from ultraviolet light. We all know that exposing skin to the sun's UV (ultraviolet) radiation damages the skin, ages it prematurely, and significantly increases the risk of skin cancer, so we know to use a lotion with an SPF of 15 or higher. I know more people will begin using coconut oil as a sunscreen when they realize how bad typical chemical-based products are for them.

High quality essential oils can be added to coconut oil for added protection as a sunscreen. It makes it even more potent. The lavender essential oil that my friend Carol, (the essential oils expert- cccforrest1@gmail.com) , uses, when mixed with coconut oil, creates an SPF of 35. Another to consider is carrot seed essential oil.

One thing I keep in mind is that everything we put on our skin is absorbed into our cells. There are so many chemical-based products to use as sunscreen. If you cannot eat something because of its toxicity, why would you put it on your skin?

USE #64   HEALS DERMATITIS

Many people do not allow themselves the self-care experience of massage therapy, or have come to me feeling embarrassed about getting a massage because of their various skin conditions. The use of essential oils with coconut oil is really good for healing most of these problems. When I have a patient with dermatitis, I put a few drops of lavender, geranium, or copaiba in my hand, and then add coconut oil to it before massaging. There are other essential oils besides these three that are especially beneficial for psoriasis and eczema, but these are the ones that I have had the most experience with.

The two most common skin disorders included in the dermatitis category are psoriasis and eczema. Sometimes, even dermatologists have difficulty telling the two apart. This is because they both share some symptoms, such as inflammation with red and itchy lesions. They both also may be brought on, or made worse, by stress and food sensitivities. One difference is that psoriasis has more of a tendency to come and go. Also, eczema seems to have more of a tendency to be weepy. But both of them respond to the same essential oils and to coconut oil. Because of its properties, it is wonderfully effective at healing both conditions.

If I had dermatitis, I would mix about a handful of coconut oil and put a few drops of an essential oil in it. Then I would rub it gently into all affected areas. If you were to do this twice per day, I am certain that you would see an improvement in your condition. If you do not have any essential oils, you can use coconut oil alone and it will help, but adding essential oils will speed up the healing process.

USE #65   SOOTHES BURNS

If you ever burn yourself or someone you know does, get some coconut oil on it right away. It will soothe the area very quickly. If you have some lavender essential oil, using a few drops of it in coconut oil will help also. Just applying coconut oil will stop the immediate pain, but when you use lavender along with it, you are sure to avoid getting blisters or scarring. Of course, this advice is not intended to replace seeking medical attention, especially if it is a severe burn.

Every day, I take a little food-grade hydrogen peroxide per my doctor's recommendations. If you've ever gotten this type of hydrogen peroxide on yourself, you will be able to relate to this. Many times I will get a drop or two on my skin somehow. It looks all white and chalky and burns like crazy. Water does not make it feel any better. So, one day, I put just a little coconut oil on it, and guess what? No pain. I am sure that using coconut oil on any condition similar to a burn will help decrease pain. At the time, I wasn't aware of adding lavender to the oil but if it ever happens again I will use it.

USE #66   ELIMINATES HALITOSIS (BAD BREATH)

If I put about a tablespoon of coconut oil in my mouth with two drops of peppermint oil and swish it around for about 15 to 20 minutes, my breath stays fresh for a long time. Then I spit it out. Not only does this help to keep my breath fresh, but, as I mentioned earlier in this book, when you swish coconut oil around in your mouth, it helps keep your gums healthy. It also helps to heal any kind of mouth sores.

There are other essential oils you can use to get your breath smelling good, but personally I like using the cool, refreshing peppermint. It has all kinds of other benefits to it, such as healing headaches, nausea, sea sickness, and clearing out the sinuses. I have heard that swishing the oil alone around in the mouth will help with bad breath, but I like to use it with peppermint oil when I am having this problem.

USE #67   RELIEVES STRESS

Who doesn't need some sort of stress relief? Every person that I massage talks about the stress in their life in one way or another. Therefore, I investigated what essential oils I can add to coconut oil to bring a patient an even greater sense of peace. The aroma of an essential oil sends specific signals to the brain and triggers an emotional reaction.

Most people respond well to the use of lavender oil for stress relief, but there are many others that are just as helpful that most people are not aware of. These include Roman Chamomile, vetiver, valerian, sandalwood, and marjoram. If you are feeling particularly stressed, or are generally a high-stress person, make sure you put a few drops of at least one of these essential oils into coconut oil and rub it into your skin. On days when things are really tense, try using it in the morning and before bed.

Put some coconut oil in your hand and add a few drops of your favorite stress relief essential oil. Now, try rubbing it on the back of your neck, or your temples, or the arch of your feet. Breathe in deeply when you do this to get the full benefits. Over time, this helps you stop using and depending on adrenaline for energy, a dangerous condition if it becomes chronic. Being chronically stressed may lead to adrenal fatigue and serious metabolism and health problems. Adopting new habits to de-stress during the day, including using a coconut/ essential oil remedy, is one of the best things you could do to improve your health right away.

USE #68   REPELS BUGS

Some people get bug bites more often than others. I am one of those people, so when I found out how you can repel bugs with coconut oil, I was really excited. Then I found out that if you add certain essential oils, it makes the solution even more powerful. Try putting a few drops of essential oil into some coconut oil and rubbing it on your skin. When I started researching this, I realized that there are many essential oils that bugs don't like. Some bugs react stronger to particular oils more than to others. The best essential oils for generally warding off bugs are citronella and lemon.

Also, remember if the bugs do get you, coconut oil is great for decreasing itchiness and inflammation. You can also keep putting on lemon essential oil, as it will help with itching as well. I have found, though, that coconut oil alone will take the itch out for me.

USE #69   SOOTHES ATHLETE'S FOOT

Please note that you can successfully use coconut oil alone in treating athlete's foot, but if you add a few drops of sandalwood essential oil, you will accelerate healing. Personally, I have never had athlete's foot, but I know of others who have, and they say it is a miserable condition.

Coconut oil will help with any irritation and itching associated with athlete's foot. When you add sandalwood, you are probably using the most effective essential oil available for this condition. It is easy to find, nice-smelling, and thought to be one of the safest oils to use.

Once you have a small handful of coconut oil, if it is thickened, you should put about three drops of sandalwood into it. If the oil has liquefied, use about one-eighth of a cup and add three drops of sandalwood essential oil. Then, rub your feet with this mixture. Wait a few minutes and it will absorb quickly. Be careful, though, not to get up too quickly, as your feet may slide out from underneath you if you don't wait until it's absorbed. Make sure you cover the whole foot, even going between the toes.

You should notice a difference in a few days. Certainly, there will be less itchiness and irritation in a short time. Keep it up, though. If you are prone to athlete's foot, you might want to make this a part of your regular foot care routine.

USE #70   HELPS YOU SLEEP

Many people experience insomnia. Actually, there was a short period of my life when I did, too. Of course, there are many things that can contribute to poor sleep, and these should always be considered. Some people have found help with natural remedies such as supplements, herbs, diet, relaxation therapies and meditation. Well, let me add a new one here.

How about massaging yourself with a mixture of coconut oil and some of the same essential oils you would use for stress relief? Try one or two of these from this list: vetiver, valerian, lavender, sandalwood, marjoram or Roman Chamomile. Make sure you breathe in deeply, allowing the aroma which is carrying the natural compounds to be inhaled through both your nose and mouth. You might want to try rubbing the mixture of coconut and essential oils up and down the arch of your feet or on your temples.

USE #71   CLEARS UP ACNE

In my late twenties, I developed adult acne. I tried everything from antibiotics to Proactive. No matter how harsh or toxic the remedy, I subjected my poor skin to it. (Am I vain, or what?) Just think of all the chemicals I used on my skin and in my body. Today, there is much written about the use of coconut oil for the treatment of acne. I sure wish I had known about it back then. It is one of the healthiest ways to get rid of acne.

If I had acne today, I would be ingesting coconut oil as well as putting it directly on the affected areas. Also, I would be putting it on any scars that appeared due to the acne. When you are treating acne, it is important to start seeing results quickly, which coconut oil will provide.

One thing you can add to coconut oil is the essential oil, lemongrass. It will help because it normalizes oil production. This, along with the anti-inflammatory properties of coconut oil, should really help to clear up this condition. It also has a nice, clean smell and is good for you instead of being a product full of chemicals that you feel are burning your skin as you apply it.

USE #72   ENDS RESPIRATORY INFECTIONS

Here's a great idea. Remember when you used to rub Vick's Vaporub on your chest? Well, you can rub coconut oil on your chest, which has a similar consistency when it's cooled. If you are congested, you can also put some of this into your nose and if you add some essential oils, it will work even more effectively.

When you make a mixture, take a handful of coconut oil and put two to three drops of the following essential oils into it—peppermint, eucalyptus, tea tree, or a mixture of any of these. Then, rub this oil on your chest, and it will absorb in very quickly. You can also try frankincense to strengthen the lungs.

USE #73   REPLACES YOUR DEODORANT

This really works. (Would I kid about body odor?!) First, what I do is I take a little coconut oil and wipe my underarms with it. After that, I take a little of the oil and rub it in (to clean skin). Bacteria that accumulates under the arms is what creates an odor. Because of its antibacterial properties, coconut oil alone is a wonderful, chemical-free deodorant.

One thing to consider is that the underarm is the perfect place to add essential oils. When your skin is warm and moist, it absorbs more readily. When you use coconut oil as a deodorant, it is the perfect opportunity to add an essential oil. Which one you chose to add is up to you. Whenever you are in doubt as to which one to use please feel free to check with my friend Carol (cccforrest1@gmail.com), who is thoroughly knowledgeable and can supply you with any essential oil you need. Most of the time, I add peppermint essential oil when using it as a deodorant. Again, using coconut oil, especially with an essential oil added, is an easy, pleasant way to substitute a natural, effective product. It can replace commercial deodorants which usually contain aluminum compounds.

USE #74   SOFTENS CRACKED SKIN

This is another use for coconut oil that I have tried. When my skin cracks, it is very painful, and the idea that I can use something that is not harmful to me is especially exciting. It is also nice to know that if it seeps in deeper into my system, it is *good* for me, as well.

Sometimes, I get cracked skin around my heels. Using coconut oil seems to almost immediately help heal the area. It feels good to rub it in with a little lavender essential oil which helps calm the area. After I am done using the oils, I am careful when I walk on the floor, so as not to slip.

Wherever your skin gets especially dry or cracked, try the coconut oil (some people use it on their elbows after every shower to keep the skin soft.)

USE #75   SUBDUES SCIATICA SYMPTOMS

If you have ever had sciatica pain, you'll definitely understand why someone suffering from it might be willing to try anything to cure it. It is horrible, and I know because I used to get it all the time. I haven't had it in years, so I have not had the need to try the coconut and essential oil mix that I am about to tell you about on myself. However, many of my patients come to me complaining of pain from sciatica, and this method seems to do the trick for them.

There are two essential oils that, when mixed with the coconut oil, have great results with sciatica pain. One of the essential oils to add is peppermint because it "cools" down the area. Once again, take a handful of coconut oil, or one-eighth of a cup if it's liquefied, and sprinkle two to three drops of peppermint into it. Then, rub the mix on the areas that hurt.

This should bring down any immediate discomfort. Another thing you can do is mix lavender in with the coconut oil alone or along with the peppermint too. They are all great anti-inflammatory oils, so this mixture should lessen the pain, too.

USE #76   COMFORTS DEMENTIA/ALZHEIMERS PATIENTS

My doctor, Dr. Monhollon, (www.floridaintegrative.com), said that a family member of his has signs of dementia. He has recommended that he ingest the oil for this condition. He has him taking seven tablespoons of coconut oil per day. Obviously, he believes in the healing powers of coconut oil.

My dad passed a few years ago at the age of 92. He had had Alzheimer's for years beforehand. I wish that I knew then what I do now about coconut oil and essential oils for this condition.

Until you have a loved one with dementia, it is difficult to know all that goes on. Most people think that it only involves the memory. That is not true. People with dementia can become combative as well as depressed. They are not able to think clearly and become easily confused. I know this because of my dad, but also because I worked as a counselor at a psychiatric hospital for nine years.

Because I also believe in the power of essential oils, I have been studying which ones would help with the various symptoms of dementia. They can easily be added to coconut oil and will help tremendously. There are documented cases on the therapeutic benefits of essential oils with dementia. Not just that, but I believe that aromas in general are healing for these patients. They stimulate parts of the brain that can bring back memories. Also, because these folks are sometimes limited socially and physically, the smells of experiences in the past can be comforting.

The best and/or most popular essential oils for addressing different symptoms of dementia are as follows:

- ▶ Frankincense: Wonderful for concentration and help in focusing.

- ▶ Lemon Balm: Great for anxiety, depression and insomnia.

- ▶ Lavender: Helps with anxiety, insomnia, memory, depression and agitation.

- ▶ Peppermint: Stimulates the appetite and mind, calms nerves and stomach upset. Helps absent-mindedness.

- ▶ Rosemary: Stimulates cognitive abilities and concentration and uplifts mood.

- ▶ Bergamot: Has a calming effect and uplifts the mood.

There are many ways to use essential oils with coconut oil. The most effective way is to combine about one-eighth of a cup of coconut oil with a few drops of one or more essential oils. Pay attention to what you can read about the therapeutic effects of each essential oil to determine when to use which one. For instance, it would be best to use lavender at night, if they have trouble sleeping.

After mixing the two oils, try rubbing the mixture on the person's arch of their foot, if you can. It might be easier, though, to rub a little on their back, neck or temples. When you use coconut oil as what is considered the "carrier oil," it is easy to get an essential oil into the bloodstream very fast. Coconut oil is good for diluting any oils that might be very strong, as well. At first, use a small amount, maybe one drop, of the essential oil to see how the person reacts. Not only will your loved one/patient respond to the therapeutic effects of these two oils, but they will most likely enjoy and benefit from your touch.

Another benefit of mixing essential oils into coconut oil is the effect coconut oil has on the skin which, in the elderly, may not be getting the TLC it should. The oil will quickly work to moisturize and soften the skin. Also, our skin becomes thinner as we age, and coconut oil is perfect for strengthening the elasticity. And remember, it will also kill off any microbes, bacteria, fungus and/or viruses that may be on the skin. There will be no harmful side effects from using a combination of these two oils. It will penetrate into the person's body and heal. I love this stuff!

USE #77   CONTROLS HEAD LICE

None of my friends will admit it when they have head lice—how about yours? I have only heard a few rare instances where adults get head lice, and I don't have children, so I have not personally experienced the horrible itching from head lice. Someone I know personally got head lice from their kindergartener. After buying the expensive product and doing the treatment on her daughter, the next night was spent repeating the whole procedure on herself. The foul-smelling, strong chemicals (literally an insecticide) was absorbed through her scalp and caused such an allergic reaction she had to go to the emergency room with severe asthma. Time to look for a natural remedy!

When you read about the benefits of coconut oil, relief from head lice bites is listed as one of them. A few people told how they would saturate their head with coconut oil, and then cover it with something like a shower cap and go to sleep. In the morning, they would wash it out and repeat a few days later. This gets rid of the lice and any "nits" (their eggs or young lice), especially with repeated application.

If I were doing this, I think I might want to add an essential oil that might make me feel cleaner. An essential oil such as tea tree or bergamot might help me feel as if I was doing everything I could do to remedy the problem. Plus, the scents of both of these oils smell clean and fresh. If you do not like these choices, there are plenty of other essential oils that may work for you. The real treatment is in leaving the coconut oil on overnight any way you can.

Chapter 7

EVEN MORE TERRIFIC
AND PRACTICAL USES

During my research and experimentation, I've found a variety of uses for coconut oil that don't seem to fit in with the others, so I am putting them into a miscellaneous category. They comprise quite an interesting group. A lot of them will surprise you, as they did me. When you start trying it for everything (TIFE), you will be amazed at all that it can do.

The other night I was at a get-together. Friends were asking me what I had been doing lately and I started telling them about writing this book. They told me that I lit up when I began telling them about coconut oil and all that it can be used for. It doesn't surprise me. I love this stuff! I love sharing with you everything I can think of which may be of value to you. Thank you for coming along with me so far—I hope you've already made a list of the ways you want to start using coconut oil right away. If you have not yet gotten your first jar, go write it on your grocery list right now!

This chapter includes some of the zaniest uses, but bear with me. When you try them, you will see what I am so excited about. Hopefully, it will encourage you to get in the TIFE mood, too. As you really understand how fantastic coconut oil is for you and your world, I'm sure you will start to find some unusual or odd uses, too. The possibilities are endless.

NOTE: As in Chapter 3, some of the uses below are health-related. Of course, these uses should not replace medical advice, diagnosis or treatment. If you have a severe injury

or condition, the need for medical attention is especially important, as soon as possible.

USE #78   BATTLES LOVE BUGS

Here's another TIFE experience. Unless you live in Florida or the South, you may not understand what a valuable use this one is. In the summer, we have a few months where "love bugs" (so called because they literally live only long enough to reproduce) fly around (coupled) and get stuck onto anything colliding with their path. They are black, and a cloud of them can literally obstruct a driver's vision before, and after, splatting on the windshield.

There's a whole long story about these guys I won't bore you with, but trust me, they are a nuisance. When you drive, hundreds of them end up on your car's grill, headlights, and hood front. They stick like they are super-glued, and require much effort to remove, not just a normal car wash and rinse. Not only that, but if left on, their body fluid residues will corrode the paint.

So, here's what I did. I took a cloth and put it into the oil, and rubbed the oil on the front of my car *before* I took a trip. And guess what? The love bugs did not stick to my car. Most of them slid right off. A rare few clung on tenaciously and were there when I got to my destination, but they came off easily with a cloth. This may not sound like a big deal to you if you've never dealt with these critters, but trust me—this use of coconut oil is a fantastic time and aggravation saver.

USE #79   PROTECTS YOUR NOSE

When sharing my enthusiasm for coconut oil with a client, I heard this great first-hand story. They were out skiing for the day, and their nose was becoming red and cracked because of the dry, cold air. They had a little coconut oil with them to use for a facial moisturizer, so they put some extra up into their nostrils, and especially around the opening, to ward off the effects of the inhospitable weather.

Usually, their nose would become red and would even form small cracks in this kind of dry, cold air exposure. It would become a distracting and sometimes painful situation while on their trip. When they applied the oil both before and after being out in the cold, however, the symptoms lessened considerably, and it became easier to enjoy being outside. New policy: never travel without coconut oil!

USE #80 SERVES AS A DECORATION

Did you know that coconut oil will freeze? And when it does, you can float it in cold liquid. I put some oil in a small, round ice ring. Then, I put food coloring in it and made it orange. Next, I put some tiny flowers with a little water in a small Dixie cup, and put it in the middle of the ring. When I put this into a large bowl of cold water, it floated and looked really pretty. What would I use it for? Honestly, I don't know, but it was fun creating it.

I'm sure if I spent more time on the decorating capabilities of coconut oil, I could come up with more because it can basically be molded into anything. The one thing that needs to be kept in mind is the fact that it changes consistency at around 76 degrees. So, for instance, if you wanted to do the decoration above, you would have to make sure the liquid it is floating in is colder than 76 degrees, so you would need to keep it cold too by putting in some ice or an ice pack.

USE #81 DEODORIZES JUST ABOUT ANYTHING

Here's a funny one—you can guess I was in a TIFE mood. The other day, after making my dogs' dinner, I was in a hurry, and I only realized after I left the house that I smelled like the fish I had just fed them. Instead of heading back home or stopping to wash my hands, I did this: I happened to have some coconut oil nearby, so I rubbed a bit into my hands and neck.

When I got to my friend's house, I braced myself for her grossed-out reaction. To my surprise, though, when I asked her, she said that I smelled good. Really? Really! I washed my hands after that, of course, but in a pinch, the oil worked like magic. Since then I have tried it on other offensive smells, just to see if it works, and it does. I love this stuff!

USE #82 TREATS MINOR INJURIES

This is one of my favorite creative, TIFE uses that I came up with. What you do is put some coconut oil in a small Dixie cup and freeze it. It will harden just like ice in about 15 minutes. My suggestion is to do this now so you will have it on hand as soon as you need it. If you don't have a Dixie cup available, try putting a little of the coconut oil in a baggie and freeze it.

Once the coconut oil has frozen, peel back about 1/2 an inch down from the top of the dixie cup. If you used a baggie instead, fold the plastic down and use this area as a way to grip the frozen oil without having to hold it directly. Now you will have a way to hold the frozen coconut oil while you are gliding it over the injury.

This is an idea I created because I am a massage therapist and am always thinking about ways to improve treatment for injuries. When you apply something cold to an injury, it brings down inflammation. Coconut oil, even when warm, reduces inflammation. Putting these two together, frozen coconut oil is doubly effective, and also works well on cuts, bruises and for preventing infection by creating a protective barrier so dirt cannot get into an injured area.

USE #83   PROTECTS HAIR

Take a small amount of coconut oil, maybe a half or whole teaspoon, according to how much hair you have. This is especially beneficial if you live in Florida, where the sun is intense and there is a lot of salt in the air. Our hair can get almost parched looking. The coconut oil creates a barrier that protects your hair.

One day when I came home, my hair was looking dried out. I had already taken a shower earlier and I was in a hurry, so I just patted a little oil into my hair. My hair looked instantly lustrous and healthy. It also helped to control that fly-away look.

USE #84   LUBRICATES A SWOLLEN RING
FINGER

Here's one you may not have thought of, but will probably wish you had at some point. It is one of those that you'll also say, "Why didn't I think of that?" It may not be a big deal, but it certainly came in handy for me.

Sometimes, when I ingest a lot of salt or have been close to the beach for any length of time, my fingers will swell. Also, if I gain even a few pounds, my fingers grow larger. Then, I find it hard to get my rings on and off. The other day I had trouble getting one of my rings off. I put some coconut oil on my finger, though, and it slipped off with no problem.

USE #85   ADDRESSES SMELLY BELLY BUTTON SYNDROME

This is an embarrassing problem. I won't go too much into detail about this problem, but I have what is called (yes, there actually is a name for it) "smelly button syndrome." If you don't believe me, do an Internet search on it. It is caused by bacteria accumulating in deep, inverted belly buttons, which causes a smell. Coconut oil, thanks to its antibacterial properties, fights off this bad smell.

Please don't laugh! Apparently, there are a lot of people with this problem who have deep inverted navels, because it is easy for things to accumulate in there. Don't ask me how I found out either. Once I did find out about it, however, I tried a lot of different things to get rid of it.

One thing I tried was putting rubbing alcohol in it. Then I tried witch hazel and various essential oils. There were other things I tried over the years, but many of them burned or itched and none of them really worked well. Nothing was helping until I started using coconut oil and decided to try applying it directly in my belly button.

What I did was to lie down on my back on my bed. Then I put a little oil in liquefied form into a dropper and squirted a few drops into my belly button. I swished it around with a Q-Tip. Then, I put a Band-Aid over it to hold it in and went to sleep. In the morning, I cleaned it out with a Q-Tip again. The next night, I did the same thing again, just to be safe.

This was a few months ago. As far as I know my "syndrome" is gone. I'm not sure if it will ever come back, but if it does, I know how to handle it.

Recently, sure enough, I heard a story from a smart mom who uses this method to keep her twin toddlers' sweaty, juice-stained belly buttons clean and healthy. Before finding this remedy, the problem was driving her crazy because the bacteria would start to cause itching which the kids would naturally scratch relentlessly with dirty nails until the "smelly" problem became an "infected" problem. She reports that the coconut oil treatment has eliminated this issue completely.

USE #86   GETS HERBS INTO YOUR SYSTEM

This may sound like a funny one, but I swallow a lot of different herbs everyday for various reasons. When I buy my herbs in bulk, it saves me some money, but then I have to put it in capsules or find another way to get it down. One day, when I was in a hurry, I mixed the herb turmeric in with coconut oil and swallowed it. It really wasn't hard to swallow, probably because coconut oil is a little sweet and I like the taste of it. Since then, I have used it to help me swallow other herbs, like white willow bark.

I'm sure this will be helpful for ingesting anything that is in powder or loose form if it is not convenient to put it into capsules. It is easiest if the oil is a little on the cool side, and therefore a thicker consistency. Then, just scoop up about a tablespoon of coconut oil, put the powder in the middle of it, and ingest it. It will be easy to swallow, regardless of what its consistency is.

USE #87   STOPS AN ITCH

Any time you have an itch, try coconut oil on it before you do anything else. Honestly, it takes the itch out of just about anything. A while ago, while writing this book, I was walking my dogs and stepped into a red ant hill. I'm not sure if they were what is considered "fire ants" but they were small and red. Usually, it feels as if they are continuing to bite me long after they have stopped, and then the intense itching begins. But I outsmarted them this time. I quickly went home and rubbed about half a teaspoon on my foot. In less than a minute, I had forgotten all about being bitten. I had absolutely no itching or any kind of lasting effect. Of course, you need to do this as soon as possible.

Then, another time, I have no idea why, but my leg was itching. There was no bug bite or sting. My skin didn't even look particularly dry. I hadn't been out in the sun, so I couldn't blame it on that, either. So, I thought "what the heck" and I rubbed some coconut oil in the area. In a few minutes, I had no itchiness. I love this stuff!

Here's one more "itch" story that will surprise you. Again, I was walking my dogs, and I started chatting with a man that I occasionally see. We started talking about what we had been up to lately, and I told him about this book. He told me he had had some sort of odd itching going down his arm, and when he went to his doctor, he told him it was a neurological response because of a nerve being pinched in the neck. Then, guess what the doctor told him? "Rub some coconut oil on it for the itching." Isn't that great? It's getting accepted into the medical community! The man told me that when he rubbed coconut oil on his arm, it really helped.

USE #88   QUIETS WASP/BEE STINGS

About 20 years ago, I found out I have a mild allergic reaction to wasp and bee stings. Since then, I always keep Benadryl handy. Just recently I got stung by a wasp and before I reached for the Benadryl I put coconut oil on it. Usually I itch pretty badly, even when I use Benadryl, but with coconut oil, I had absolutely no itching afterwards. This is huge for me. Also, there wasn't any stinging after about five minutes.

When I first had an allergic reaction to being stung, I developed this strange rash. My throat closed off a little, too. It was pretty scary. I was told to never go out without having Benadryl handy, in case I ever got stung again, which I did.

The idea of not using the Benadryl if I ever get stung again is really uncomfortable for me. I can see myself using coconut oil for the topical reaction, but I probably will never completely stop myself from taking Benadryl. If you want to try using coconut oil for this, I recommend doing the same—it's a big help, but don't use it to completely replace whatever your doctor recommends.

USE #89   REPLACES ULTRASOUND GEL

As I've mentioned, I am a neuromuscular massage therapist. There have been times in my career when I have had to perform ultrasound therapy on a patient. If you are not familiar with what I am talking about, the sort of ultrasound we use is for sending sound waves into an area to speed healing. Ultrasound is also used a lot in chiropractor's offices, though it is not the same ultrasound that is used to see an unborn baby in a mother's belly.

When you do a treatment with ultrasound, you first apply an electrode gel substance to glide the machine. The gel also acts as a conduit. I started thinking about the properties of coconut oil and wondered why I couldn't use it in place of the ultrasound gel. So, I slathered a lot of the oil on my arm and began moving the ultra sound head around on my skin, just as I would do if I were using the commercial gel. It worked beautifully and had a more pleasing smell. And remember, the anti-inflammatory properties in the coconut oil can help the healing process along with the sound waves.

USE #90   REMOVES ADHESIVES/PAINT

Is there anything with a more sharp and repugnant smell than paint or glue remover? Maybe you'll never have to hold your nose for that stuff again! Just the other day I was massaging someone with coconut oil. When I got to her thigh, I noticed she had a big white blotch on her leg. I asked her what it was from, and she said she wasn't sure because she couldn't see it. Also, she said she had been working around the house and it could be a number of things, but most likely it was paint. As I kept massaging with the oil, I noticed that the paint blotch began just disintegrating. From this experience, I got an idea.

When I got home I decided to see what else the oil could do in regard to removing adhesives. I had some leftover glue on my skin from a Band-Aid that I had taken off recently. You guessed it—coconut oil lifted the sticky goo right off my skin. Then I remembered that I had, for some unknown reason, put a piece of scotch tape just below my dashboard a while back. I'm sure I must have had a reason for this, but I can't remember what it was. Anyway, there it was, very securely

74

glued to the side of my gear shift. After I put some of the oil on it, it lifted right off.

Coconut oil softens all kinds of things so beautifully, not just the skin. As you will probably notice, if you use it for this kind of application, it will lift just about anything off. It won't work on enamel-based products that have adhered to certain surfaces, such as fingernails, though.

Besides its ability to remove adhesives, you don't have to worry about applying toxic chemicals to your skin or your items. You also don't have to breathe in the chemical fumes. Great stuff, this miracle of nature!

USE #91   ENCOURAGES HAIR GROWTH

I wasn't sure whether to put this in the health or the beauty section because it really is both, so I put it here. Please forgive me if you have been looking elsewhere for this popular topic. This great benefit of coconut oil should make a lot of people happy.

One of the reasons that the oil helps with hair growth is that it goes deep into the hair follicles. Damaged areas of the body will blossom if given healthy nutrients, but you have to make sure they are able to be absorbed. Coconut oil penetrates deep into tissues and cells.

My hair has thickened since I started regularly ingesting coconut oil. Since I do not have any problems with hair loss, I have not had a reason to massage it into the scalp, other than just to condition my hair. If I was losing hair, I would make sure I ingested it as well as massaging it into my scalp on a daily basis.

USE #92   DECREASES DANDRUFF

There are a whole lot of people who suffer from dandruff. If you are a dandruff sufferer, especially if it is extreme, you have to watch what you wear, because it shows up on darker colors. You have to make sure you are not scratching at it in public, as well. You have to make sure there are no dandruff leftovers in your fingernails after you've been scratching. On top of all that, dandruff shampoos are generally more expensive and not as accessible as regular varieties, and they don't always work.

Coconut oil, in general, promotes scalp health. It naturally conditions and strengthens your hair and scalp. But, beyond this, it is anti-fungal and dandruff is a fungus.

Here's what you do: slather some coconut oil into your scalp before you go to bed. Put a shower cap or even a plastic bag around your head to keep the oil on your scalp, not on your pillow. When you get up in the morning, wash it out with cool water. A too-warm shower will further aggravate the situation, as the warmth will dry out the area. If it doesn't help the first time you do it, keep going through this process a few more times. It should really help.

USE #93   CONTROLS TOPICAL YEAST
INFECTIONS

Any kind of topical yeast infection should be able to be controlled with coconut oil. This is because it is anti-fungal. Personally, I have not had any experience with this but I know there are people out there with odd, unexplained spots on their skin who might benefit from this.

If you have a recurring spot on your skin of an unknown nature, it may be a topical yeast infection. A couple of months ago I had someone come to me for a massage who was complaining about a spot on their back. The only kind of oil I use now when I massage is coconut oil. I put some extra oil on the affected spot for them, and they said it went away in the next day or so.

One word of warning: if you have any unexplained, odd-shaped or odd-colored dark spots or moles on your skin, please see your doctor right away. In fact, any time you have any unexplained spot on your skin, make sure you get it checked out to eliminate the possibility it could be pre-cancerous or cancerous. It is not worth the risk you will take if you don't find out what it is.

USE #94 BENEFITS YOUR PET'S HEALTH

The health benefits of coconut oil aren't just for humans. My dogs love coconut oil. In fact, everyone I know that has a dog says that their dog loves it. It is good for them for some of the same reasons that it is good for humans.

A friend of mine, Susan, tried using it on her cat. Her cat had some abrasions on her and she was using the oil as a wound dressing. She is not sure how the cat feels about it. Unsurprisingly, the cat didn't seem too happy about having oil in its fur, but it did seem to help with the wounds, at least.

Look at the health benefits of coconut oil for humans, and you will undoubtedly read about something that you can use the oil on for your pet. My dogs ingest about two tablespoons per day. I give them coconut oil for many reasons. It is good for their heart health, inflammation, parasites, infection—well, you name it. They need it.

I started giving them two tablespoons per day about three months ago. Also, when I need to give them a pill or supplement, I can hide it in coconut oil when it is in its hardened form. Their energy levels have definitely improved and their coats are shiny and healthy.

Below this are a few more ideas for using the oil for your critters.

USE #95   CONTROLS YOUR PET'S ITCHY/HOT SPOTS

My dogs sometimes get unknown itchy spots on them, so I thought, "What the heck, I'll try it on them—it helps my itchy spots, why not theirs?" And it does help, if I can keep it on them without them licking it all off. They love the taste of coconut oil. I'm sure your dogs will do the same. Maybe if you added an essential oil that they don't love the taste of, it will stop them from licking it off. I'm going to try that next time.

Once again, probably because it decreases inflammation, coconut oil decreases itching. If the itching has been brought on by something viral, parasitic or fungal, the oil will address this. It would be good to have them eat some, too. Believe me, if they are like my dogs, they will love it.

USE # 96   SUPPLIES OUR DOGS WITH A HEALTHY TREAT

You can use coconut oil to replace commercial dog biscuits. What I do is put about a tablespoon in each section of an ice cube tray and freeze it. They pop out easily when frozen. My dogs love to crunch these down. Again, I'm not sure how cats feel about all this coconut stuff, but it couldn't hurt to try.

When they eat this treat it is benefitting them in many ways. Of course, this is aside from the pure pleasure of it. They are getting all the health advantages of the coconut oil which is, a lot of times, more than what regular dog treats supply. This list includes better digestion, healthy gums, getting rid of parasites, supplying them with antioxidants, amongst other benefits. On top of all this, it is a lot less expensive than regular dog treats.

USE # 97   CLEANS DOGS' EARS

You can use the oil to clean dogs' ears because it is antibacterial and antimicrobial. If their ears are pink inside, it is probably due to an infection or inflammation. It could also be from parasites. Coconut oil will address all of these issues. How much money would you save from a vet visit and prescription ear drops if coconut oil solved this problem for your dog?

Sometimes, when I haven't cleaned my dogs' ears in a while, I give them a really good cleaning. First, I put one-two tablespoons of coconut oil down each ear. Then I rub it in, especially at the base of the ear, for about one minute. After that, I get out of their way and let the dog shake its head. When they have stopped, I clean the oil out with a dry cloth and then go in with a few Q- Tips to get in crevices.

Did you notice I didn't include cats here? That's because I don't have cats. I imagine that it will be much more difficult to do this with your cat but the advantages would be the same.

USE #98   REDUCES CRADLE CAP

Cradle cap is a type of dermatitis, called infantile seborrheic dermatitis, which is very common. It can look like dandruff with flaky, dry skin. It can also look like thick, oily crusting patches. Either way, it may also be on other parts of the body besides the head, especially the face.

This is one use that I read about many times over. There are not any babies around me, so I have not tried it yet either. I would not hesitate to try it on my baby's head, because if it doesn't help, it will not harm, since it is nontoxic. It will soften the skin and address any problems associated with cradle cap. Try putting a little on the scalp and leaving it on overnight. Brush the scalp in the morning with a soft brush.

USE #99   SOOTHES NIPPLE SORENESS FROM BREAST-FEEDING

This is a problem I was not aware of because I've never had children. Someone told me about their experience. It is probably not something everyone talks about, but in my profession as a massage therapist, I never know what people will tell me.

Once I heard about this, I did some research and found it is a very common complaint, and also read about how some women have to reluctantly give up breast feeding because it is just too painful. I hope you will help spread the word, share this book, and tell your OB/GYN to let women know they should give coconut oil a try.

It would probably be easier to apply it if the consistency of the oil was a little on the cool side, so it was more like a lotion. Rub it gently into the area as often as you can. It should start to resolve this problem in days, if not sooner. It is best to keep the nipple from drying and cracking in the first place, so the oil should be used from the start. The great thing about coconut oil is, of course, that it is not going to harm the baby if some of it gets in its mouth. In fact, the high amounts of lauric acid that are in the coconut oil are what is also in mother's milk!

USE #100 STOPS DIAPER RASH

Itchy, red, irritated skin is never so deserving of sympathy than when it's on a sweet little baby's butt.It just hurts to look at it, especially when powders and creams are so ineffective. Attention mommy-bloggers! Let everyone know about using coconut oil when there is diaper rash. Isn't it nice to know that you can address this problem without the use of chemicals or products that block pores? Just rubbing coconut oil directly but gently on your baby is all you need to do.

USE #101 REPLACES OR COMBINES WITH BUTTER

One of my friends, Julia, told me she does this next one. She says she loves the taste of real butter, so she doesn't want to give it up altogether. What she does instead is to take equal parts coconut oil and mix it with real butter, whip them together and put them back in the fridge. Then she uses the mix as she would butter. When I asked her why she did this she said it's because of the health benefits that coconut oil provides.

Though it depends on where you get your information, some opinions regarding the consumption of butter, do vary. Remember that butter has saturated fat, just like coconut oil, but the fat in butter is derived from animal, whereas the fat in coconut oil is plant based. This difference is what some health experts are saying makes the difference. Both butter and coconut oil provide almost the same amount of calories, too—102 for butter and 117 for coconut oil. One thing is for sure, the other substitutes for butter are loaded with unhealthy ingredients.

USE #102 (OH NO! WAIT! I'VE GOT ONE MORE USE!!!) SERVES AS A GREAT GIFT!

What could be better than giving friends and family the gift of health? And doesn't everyone love a practical and useful gift? Coconut oil comes in containers that are perfect to give as gifts. Won't it make you feel good to contribute to your loved ones' health and happiness? Packaging this book, *101 Creative Coconut Oil Uses*, with some coconut oil will surely please people who know, or don't yet know, about coconut oil.

Chapter 8

TIPS ABOUT COCONUT OIL

► One person I know that does oil pulling says that she is reluctant to spit it into the drain. She is worried that it will become cool and harden, causing future build up in her pipes. This may be true especially if you live in a cooler climate and are using it on a daily basis.

► Buy organic, virgin, unrefined coconut oil if you don't mind the taste.

► If you dislike the taste or smell of the more pure form, you can purchase refined coconut oil, which has no scent to it. Some people say it doesn't have as many health benefits to it, but I haven't yet found any data supporting that.

► It changes consistency at about 76 degrees, so when you want it in a liquefied form, leave it on your counter top or put in a bowl in a pan of warm water for a few minutes. When you want to harden it place it in the freezer for about five minutes.

► Keep it covered if you leave it out.

► Start out ingesting less and gradually increasing the dosage. Most people can handle one tablespoon. Lessen the amount if you experience diarrhea. As your body adjusts, you may find you can ingest more later.

▶ If you give it to your pets wait and see if they get diarrhea and if so, back off the amount. Base the amount you start off with on the size of your pet. I have three large dogs and I started them on a teaspoon per day and they now ingest two tablespoons per day.

▶ Keep your coconut oil out of direct sunlight.

▶ Consider coconut oil as a food. There are a lot of people who consume five tablespoons per day with no adverse affects and others who are only able to eat one tablespoon per day, so it varies from person to person, just as other foods.

▶ A friend of mine, Mary, who works in a health food store says customers are very interested in coconut oil but ask her all the time how to get into their system. The recipe section that you can link to has a list of suggestions for making sure you are consuming enough coconut oil.

▶ Gradually add the coconut oil into your diet. Most people start out with one teaspoon and increase from there.

▶ If you experience diarrhea you may be taking too much so try backing off on your amount and try increasing later when your body has adjusted.

▶ If you use a lot of coconut oil on your body, make sure you keep that into account when keeping track of how much coconut oil you are using.

► Although I have never tried it, supposedly you can make your own coconut oil. Go to www. wikihow.com and search "make coconut oil" or go to www.youtube.com and put in a search for "coconut oil." You can actually watch them demonstrate how to make coconut oil on Youtube.

► Virgin, unrefined coconut oil is the least processed.

► Organic coconut oil means that no chemicals have been used in either the growing of the trees or in the extraction process.

► Coconut oil can replace many different oils and even butter in most recipes. I have found that you can use equal amounts when substituting.

Remember that coconut oil lubricates, disinfects, cleans, moisturizes, softens, shines, heals, conditions, protects, nourishes, odorizes and soothes.

So get some soon and Try It For Everything!

CONCLUSION

This is quite a list of uses, isn't it? I sincerely hope you give at least some of these a try. Show coconut oil the respect it deserves!

I have really had fun compiling this list. Coconut oil is so versatile. It's truly amazing knowing all the things you can do with it. I am sure you will come up with some of your own, as well.

Our society has been so influenced by marketing. We think we need to buy and use chemicals in order to REALLY take care of our bodies and items. It obviously just isn't so. Since coconut oil can take the place of so many products, there is little need to use chemicals.

As you have read, there is also no need to stay attached to many medications and ways that we have been taught of caring for our bodies. Until I found out about coconut oil, I was limited in my options for what to use. Now I know about all the healthy aspects of the oil and I have more choices with its versatile attributes. Now you do, too!

The most fun that I have been having with coconut oil, though, involves finding uses that have never been considered. This includes uses like conditioning the vinyl and leather of your car, or shining up your candles. Someday, I may investigate other fun projects for example, creating a party centered around the use of coconut oil.

When we begin to integrate healthier and less expensive alternatives into our environment, we are taking the high road. Just think of the impact we could make if we all said no to noxious chemical products. Wouldn't you feel good to know that you played a part in this transition?

Daily use of coconut oil opens up a more liberated, expansive world to us. It is a world where doctors, pharmaceutical companies and chemical product manufacturers are less in control. Since you have been given options in this book about replacing some of these items, the responsibility of what you choose is now up to you. Before reading this book you probably weren't aware of some of your choices. Now you are—please make the healthier choice.

Enjoy!

THANK YOU FOR PURCHASING MY BOOK!
WOULD YOU PLEASE DO ME A FAVOR?

Would you go back to where you bought this book and leave your feedback? This will help me to make the next edition even better. It may also help me to know I have helped you in some way! I would appreciate it!

ABOUT THE AUTHOR

Jean Olsen has been a licensed massage therapist in the state of Florida since 1995 (FL- MA18257). She is also a certified neuromuscular therapist and a certified Emotional Freedom Technique (EFT) therapist. She has created and developed the kit, ebook and vook *Headache Free...Naturally* (www.achyhead.com).

Jean has taken classes on different subjects and has received training in aromatherapy, reflexology, nutrition, acupressure, energy healing and various massage techniques including Swedish, medical, seated, orthopedic and polarity. Other areas she has studied are: meditation, diagnostics, mind-body connection, spiritual modalities, applied kinesiology, Bach flower remedies, Feldenkrais, hypnosis, psychosomatics, neurosomatics, soft-tissue therapy and posturology and Emotional Freedom Technique.

Because of her interest in the health field, she is always researching new modalities, products and anything that has to do with healing. Her research as a massage therapist has helped her to educate others who are in different fields and/or don't have the time or inclination to study health-oriented topics. In the past, she has only been able to reach a small group of people, her clients, family and friends. Today, she has found the use of writing books to be a wonderful means to give more people bottom-line information.

There are two other books that she is proud to say, convey succinct, cutting-edge information. Her book, *Headache Free... Naturally*, was her first book, and it is revised periodically. It contains information on how to release headaches with a unique, natural easy to follow program. Her soon-to-bereleased third book, *Mastering the 7 Secrets of Massage Therapy*, is a wonderful tool for assessing whether you or a loved one will be successful in this field. It is also great for struggling therapists who need help in getting their career going. It includes a special report on how to make money marketing yourself, as well.

As a massage therapist, she is always open to different ways of helping people. Most of her life has been dedicated to this practice. This is how she continues to keep her business growing and expanding, not to mention the fact that she loves teaching others what she learns. When she finds out about new products or modalities, she shares them with her clients, family and friends. Jean really enjoys sharing what she knows. She states: "It is especially beneficial for everyone to know about all the different uses of coconut oil."

"Teaching people to help themselves has always been my passion."

SUGGESTED PLACES FOR
MORE INFORMATION

The Shocking and Surprising Secrets of Coconut Oil
by Diabetickitchen.com

The Coconut Oil Miracle
by Bruce Fife. C.N., N.D.

www.coconutresearchcenter.org

www.coconutoilfacts.org

Search the following sites for various topics regarding
coconut oil

www.ezinearticles.com

www.youtube.com

www.wikihow.com

www.doctoroz.com

REMEMBER TO CHECK OUT
MY SPECIAL GIFT TO YOU!

Visit my web site at http://jeanolsen.com for

20 DELICIOUS COCONUT OIL RECIPES